Cambridge Practice Tests for First Certificate
1

24
8°
7^b
1°

Cambridge Practice Tests for First Certificate 1

Paul Carne
Louise Hashemi and
Barbara Thomas

CAMBRIDGE
UNIVERSITY PRESS

PUBLISHED BY THE PRESS SYNDICATE OF THE UNIVERSITY OF CAMBRIDGE
The Pitt Building, Trumpington Street, Cambridge CB2 1RP, United Kingdom

CAMBRIDGE UNIVERSITY PRESS
The Edinburgh Building, Cambridge CB2 2RU, United Kingdom
40 West 20th Street, New York, NY 10011–4211, USA
10 Stamford Road, Oakleigh, Melbourne 3166, Australia

First published 1996
Fourth printing 1997

Printed in the United Kingdom at the University Press, Cambridge

ISBN 0 521 49895 3 Student's Book
ISBN 0 521 49897 X Teacher's Book
ISBN 0 521 49896 1 Self-study edition
ISBN 0 521 49898 8 Cassettes

Contents

Thanks

We are grateful to Jeanne McCarten, Elizabeth Sharman, Amanda Ogden and Peter Ducker of CUP for their hard work in helping us; to everyone at AVP Recording Studio and to all the people at UCLES who provided us with information.

The authors and publishers would also like to thank the teachers and students at the following institutions for piloting the material for us:

The Cheltenham School of English; The Bell Language School, Saffron Walden; The British Institute, Paris; Basil Paterson College, Edinburgh; Anglo Continental, Bournemouth; The British Institute, Florence; International House, Barcelona; Oxford House College, London.

Acknowledgements

The publishers are grateful to the following for permission to reproduce copyright material. It has not always been possible to identify sources of all the material used, and in such cases the publishers would welcome information from the copyright owners.

The Guardian/Observer for the articles on p.5 (*Life* magazine 3.4.94) and p.57 (*The Guardian* April 1986); New Crane Publishing Ltd for the article on p.6 (*Sainsbury's Magazine* March 1994); Lands' End Direct Merchants UK Ltd for the article on p.8 (October 1994) © Lands' End, Inc. All rights reserved; The Consumers' Association; Gruner + Jahr UK for the extracts from *Focus* magazine on p.17 (January 1994), p.19 (November 1993), p.75 (April 1993), p.94 (September 1994) and p96 (April 1993); Harrington Kilbride Publishing Group plc for the article on p.31 (*Healthcare* Spring 1994); *The Independent* for the article on p.32 (from BBC serves up a celebrity ace for Grandstand viewers by David Lister 22.2.94); Richard Ehrlich for the article on p.34 (originally published in *She* magazine) © David Ehrlich; Phoenix Publishing and Media Limited for the article on pp.37-38 (*Essentially America* Summer 1994); David Higham Associates for the extract on p.43 (from *Mr Pye* by Mervin Peake 1975); Moorland Publishing Co. Ltd for the extract on p.49 (from *Visitor's Guide to Hampshire and the Isle of Wight* by John Barton 1990); Writers News Ltd for the article on p.58 (*Writing* Magazine Spring 1994); BBC Worldwide Publishing for the Go wild! extract on p.63 (*BBC Holidays* March 1994) and the article on p.89 (*BBC Vegetarian Good Food*); The Youth Hostels Association for the Win a Fabulous Holiday extract on p.64 (*Triangle* magazine Autumn 1993); John Boswell Associates for the extract on p.71 (from *The Complete Book of Long-distance and Competitive Cycling* by Tom Doughty, published by Simon and Schuster 1983); Julie Davidson for the article on pp.84-5 (*Infusion* magazine Spring 1994), printed with the kind permission of the Tea Council); Visual Imagination Ltd for the article by Judy Sloane on p.86 (*Film Review* No. 6); Reed Consumer Books Ltd for the extract on p.100 (from *New Ideas for Family Meals* by Louise Steele 1988).

Photographs: Tony Stone Images (p.9); London Stansted Airport (p.11); Bridgeman Art Library (p.34); Ace Photo Agency (p.37); Ronald Grant Archive (p.86).
Drawings by Leslie Marshall (pp.13, 65, 90).

Colour Paper 5 Section: Photographs by J. Pembrey (1A, 2A, 2C, 2D, 4E); ZEFA (1B, 2B, 1C, 1D, 3B, 4A, 4D); N. Luckhurst (2E: T-shirt, Shakespeare book, football strip, calendar, 4B); Mirror Syndication International (2E: kilt); The Image Bank (2E: pullover; Twinings tea); John Birdsall (2F, 2G, 2H, 2I); Ace Photo (3A, 4C); Tony Stone Worldwide (3C); Rex Features (3D). Drawings by Leslie Marshall (1.5E) and Shaun Williams (3.5E).

Book design by Peter Ducker MSTD

To the student

The practice papers in this book are modelled on the papers of the University of Cambridge Local Examinations Syndicate (UCLES) **First Certificate in English** (FCE).

What is FCE?

The best-known group of Cambridge examinations for students of English as a foreign language are:

CPE – Certificate of Proficiency in English   (very advanced)
CAE – Certificate in Advanced English
FCE – First Certificate in English
PET – Preliminary English Test
KET – Key English Test   (elementary)

As you see, FCE is in the middle of the group. Passing FCE means that you are an 'independent user' of English. This means that you can use English with confidence in a variety of situations, even though you still have more to learn.

Using this book

You can use the practice tests in this book, with help from your English teacher, to:
- Judge the level of FCE to see whether it is the right examination for you.
- Get used to the kind of questions that you may meet in FCE, so that you can improve your accuracy and speed.
- Find out which papers you need most practice in.

These practice tests

This book contains four complete practice tests. Each test has five papers, like this:

Paper 1   **Reading** (1 hour 15 minutes)

Each paper contains **four texts** taken from different newspapers, magazines, books and leaflets. There are **thirty-five questions** of different kinds, including multiple choice and multiple matching.
For examples, see pp. 4–12.

Paper 2   **Writing** (1 hour 30 minutes)

Part 1: You **must answer** this section. You have to read some written material which gives information you need in your answer. You then write a **letter** of 120–180 words.
Part 2: You must **choose one** out of four writing tasks, and write 120–180 words. One of these tasks is about a book. The set books change every two

years but here are some examples of the kinds of books which might appear.
(Contact UCLES for the current list of set books – address on p.3.)
The Go-Between by L. P. Hartley (simplified version)
Jamaica Inn by Daphne du Maurier (simplified version)
Brave New World by Aldous Huxley (Longman Bridge/Longman Fiction)
Crime Never Pays Oxford Bookworm Collections (OUP)
An Inspector Calls by J. B. Priestley
For examples of Paper 2 questions, see pp. 13–16.

Paper 3   Use of English (1 hour 15 minutes)

You must answer all **five parts** of this paper. There are **sixty-five questions** and
all the answers are very short. This paper tests your knowledge of English
grammar, spelling and vocabulary, so accuracy is essential.
For examples, see pp. 17–23.

Paper 4   Listening (about 40 minutes)

The listening test is recorded on tape and is divided into **four parts**. You have to
answer all **thirty questions**. Each text is heard **twice**. There are pauses on the
tape for you to read the questions and mark your answers. There are different
kinds of questions for each part.
For examples, see pp. 24–28.

Paper 5   Speaking (about 15 minutes)

You take part in a conversation with another candidate and an examiner. There
is another examiner in the room who does not join in the conversation. During
the test the examiner will give you photographs and other pictures to look at
and talk about. Some of your conversation will be with the other candidate,
some with the examiner.

Beyond the classroom

Try to get as much practice as you can in English. Here are some suggestions to
help your studies in your own time.

Reading: Look out for English language magazines on subjects that interest you.
You may be surprised how much you understand!
Many English publishers produce simplified novels and short stories for
students of English as a foreign language. These are at different levels of
difficulty. Try reading some of these and perhaps other books in English
too. Modern thrillers are often good to start with. Above all, aim to
increase your reading speed and vocabulary.

Writing: If you have time, keep a daily diary in English; if not, what about once
a week? Get a penfriend somewhere in the English-speaking world, or
persuade a fellow student to exchange letters regularly. Whenever you
can, practise writing in English, so that you are used to it.

Listening: If you are not in an English-speaking country, find out about English-
language broadcasts in your area. Write to the BBC at Bush House, PO

Box 76, Strand, London WC2B 4PH, for details of their programmes in your part of the world. There may also be broadcasts from countries such as the USA or Australia which you can receive. If you enjoy music, look out for recordings of songs in English which have the words supplied with them. If you watch videos, try to get English-language versions of films.

Speaking: Try to practise speaking English as often as you can with your fellow students and with any English speakers you meet. You'll be surprised how much you can improve your spoken English through using it regularly.

Results

You will get a certificate when you pass the examination, showing your grade: A, B or C. A is the highest grade. You will also be informed if you do particularly well in any individual paper. D and E are failing grades. If you fail, you will be informed about which papers were your weakest.

Further information

For details about Cambridge examinations for students of English as a foreign language, write to:

EFL Division
UCLES
1 Hills Road
Cambridge
CB1 2EU
England.

Practice Test 1

PAPER 1   READING (1 hour 15 minutes)

*You are going to read a newspaper article about children's safety. Choose the most suitable heading from the list (**A–I**) for each part (**1–7**) of the article. There is one extra heading which you do not need to use. There is an example at the beginning (**0**).*
*Mark your answers **on the separate answer sheet**.*

A	Dangers off the road too
B	Trial period
C	Not what it appears to be
D	Dangerous driving
E	Dangers of fuel
F	First of many?
G	Learning to judge
H	Funds from industry
I	Danger in the city

Crash courses

0	*I*

It is a typical urban scene. Two cars are parked close together at the kerbside and a child is attempting to cross the road from between them. Down the street, another car looms. Houses flank the pavements and around the corner there is a brightly-lit petrol station.

1	

It is all extraordinarily realistic, but it is unreal. For the difference between this and thousands of similar locations throughout the country is that this street is indoors – it is a mock-up designed by studio set-builders from Anglia Television.

2	

We are standing inside a converted warehouse in Milton Keynes, home of a project which is the blueprint for an exciting new way of teaching children safety awareness, especially road safety. It is called Hazard Alley. If the centre proves successful and, having visited it, I am convinced it will, then its imaginative approach could easily be copied throughout the country.

3	

The project was started by the local authority in conjunction with the police. The finance came from commercial sponsorship by companies including Coca-Cola, Volkswagen and Anglia TV. There is already a catchy cartoon character mascot for the centre: Haza, the Hazard Alley cat.

4	

A novel setting for children to be taught and practise a wide range of safety topics, Hazard Alley takes its name from the dark alleyway in the centre of the converted warehouse which links the urban street scene and a series of country sets that focus on rural safety. As well as road drill, children are tutored in home safety and how to avoid trouble in playgrounds, parks, alleyways, near railways and on farmland.

5	

In the street scene, children practise the safe way to cross a road, including coping with parked vehicles, and are given a practical understanding of how long it takes a car to stop when travelling at 30 mph. Could the car they see looming down the road stop in time if a child stepped out between the parked cars? No, it would be through that wall at the end before it finished braking, 23 metres after the driver started to brake.

6	

On the mock-up petrol station forecourt, provided by Shell, the youngsters learn the dangers when filling a vehicle with petrol. They discuss car fires, the flammability of different components, why the car's engine must be switched off and why smoking and using a car phone are illegal on a garage forecourt.

7	

Hazard Alley is gearing up for its official opening, and the local schools which have experienced it so far have been testing out the centre before it launches into a full programme of group visits. It is already proving immensely popular. Eventually it may open to individual family groups. When that happens, it will be well worth a day trip: children will love it and they could learn something which may save their lives.

You are going to read a magazine article about being liked. For questions **8–15**, choose the answer (**A**, **B**, **C** or **D**) which you think fits best according to the text. Mark your answers **on the separate answer sheet**.

LOVE ME DO!

I've just got to talk about this problem I'm having with my postman. It all began a year ago, after the birth of his first child. Not wanting to appear rude, I asked him about the baby. The next week, not wanting him to think I had asked out of mere politeness the week before, I asked all about the baby again. Now I can't break the habit. I freeze whenever I see him coming. The words 'How's the baby?' come out on their own. It's annoying. It holds me up. It holds him up. So why can't I stop it?

The answer, of course, is that I want him to like me. Come to think of it, I want everyone to like me. This was made clear to me the other day. I found myself in the bank, replying 'Oh, as it comes' when the cashier asked how I'd like the money. Even as she was handing me the £20 note, I realised I'd have no small change with which to buy my newspaper. But, not wanting her to dislike me (she'd already written '1 x £20' on the back of my cheque), said nothing.

In order to get the £20 note down to a decent, paper-buying size, I went into the grocer's. Not wanting to buy things I didn't actually need (I do have some pride, you know), I bought some large cans of beans and a frozen chicken for dinner that night. That got the price up to a respectable £5.12, which I duly paid. I then bought my paper at the station with my hard-gained £5 note.

With my sister, it wasn't the postman who was the problem, but the caretaker of her block of flats: 'All he ever does is moan and complain; he talks at me rather than to me, never listens to a word I say, and yet for some reason I'm always really nice to him. I'm worried in case I have a domestic crisis one day, and he won't lift a finger to help.'

I have a friend called Stephen, who is a prisoner of the call-waiting device he has had installed on his phone. 'I get this beeping sound to tell me there's another call on the line, but I can never bring myself to interrupt the person I'm talking to. So I end up not concentrating on what the first person's saying, while at the same time annoying the person who's trying to get through.'

What about at work? Richard Lawton, a management trainer, warns: 'Those managers who are actually liked by most of their staff are always those to whom being liked is not the primary goal. The qualities that make managers popular are being honest with staff, treating them as

human beings and observing common courtesies like saying hello in the morning.' To illustrate the point, Richard cites the story of the company chairman who desperately wanted to be liked and who, after making one of his managers redundant, said with moist eyes that he was so, so sorry the man was leaving. To which the embittered employee replied: 'If you were that sorry, I wouldn't be leaving.' The lesson being, therefore, that if you try too hard to be liked, people won't like you.

The experts say it all starts in childhood. 'If children feel they can only get love from their parents by being good,' says Zelda West-Meads, a marriage guidance consultant, 'they develop low self-confidence and become compulsive givers.' But is there anything wrong in being a giver, the world not being exactly short of takers? Anne Cousins believes there is. 'There is a point at which giving becomes unhealthy,' she says. 'It comes when you do things for others but feel bad about it.'

I am now trying hard to say to people 'I feel uncomfortable about saying this, but ...', and tell myself 'Refusal of a request does not mean rejection of a person' and I find I can say almost anything to almost anyone.

8   Why does the writer ask the postman about his baby?
    A He is interested in the baby.
    B He wants to create a good impression.
    C The postman is always polite to him.
    D The postman enjoys a chat.

9   The writer went into the grocer's so that
    A he had some food for dinner that night.
    B he could buy a newspaper there.
    C he could ask for £20 in change.
    D he could buy something to get some change.

10   What do we find out about the writer's sister and the caretaker?
    A She doesn't want to risk offending him.
    B She doesn't pay attention to him.
    C He refuses to help her.
    D He asks her for advice.

11   How does Stephen feel about his call-waiting equipment?
    A He gets annoyed when it interrupts him.
    B He is unable to use it effectively.
    C He finds it a relief from long conversations.
    D He doesn't think it works properly.

12   Managers are more likely to be popular if they
    A help staff with their problems.
    B make sure the staff do not lose their jobs.
    C encourage staff to be polite to each other.
    D do not make too much effort to be liked.

13   When is it wrong to be 'a giver'?
    A when it makes you ill
    B when it does not give you pleasure
    C when you make other people unhappy
    D when you are unable to take from others

14   What do we learn from this article?
    A If you tell the truth, it will not make people like you less.
    B If you take time to talk to people, they will like you better.
    C You should avoid unpleasant situations where possible.
    D You shouldn't refuse other people's requests for help.

15   Why was this article written?
    A to analyse the kinds of conversations people have
    B to persuade people to be more polite to each other
    C to encourage people to have more self-confidence
    D to suggest ways of dealing with difficult people

PART 3

*You are going to read a magazine article about a woman who goes gliding. Seven paragraphs have been removed from the article. Choose from the paragraphs (**A–H**) the one which fits each gap (**16–21**). There is one extra paragraph which you do not need to use. There is an example at the beginning (**0**).*
*Mark your answers **on the separate answer sheet**.*

IN PERSON

Twelve months ago, it was Lyn Ferguson who had the honour of cutting the ribbon to declare our Oakham Distribution Centre and offices open.

0	*H*

'I had my first glider flight when I was sixteen, but it wasn't until January 1986 that I took it up seriously. My boys had gone to school, I had lots of spare time and I thought, 'What am I going to do?' It just so happened that I had the opportunity to go up in a glider as a passenger to see if I liked it. I did.'

16	

'Really, it's very easy. All you need is coordination. The average person needs about 60 flights before they can go solo, completely alone, which sounds a lot, but the average instruction flight only takes around eight minutes, so training doesn't take long. I once did eleven trips in a day when I was training.'

17	

'Well, once you've done it alone, you can register with the British Gliding Association, then work towards your Bronze Badge. Each badge after that is about height, distance and endurance.

18	

Then, there are 10 km flights (straight out and back to the beginning), and 300 km flights, which show navigation skills. They're flown in a triangle starting and finishing at the airfield.'

19	

'Once, when I was in Australia, I lost height whilst attempting a 300 km flight and had to select a field to land in. Luckily, I spotted a field with a tractor in it and was able to land there. I think the farmer was pretty surprised when a glider suddenly landed next to him! He did let me use his phone, though.'

20	

'When you have a student who's finding things difficult, you convince them that they can do it. When they do, they're so pleased with themselves. When you land and they say "I can do it", it's brilliant.'

21	

'Flying is the main part, but there are other angles too. Gliding is like everything else. What you put in is what you get out. It's all about team work too. Everybody mucks in to push gliders around, pull cables in and generally help out. You can't do it on your own. I've met people in gliding from all walks of life, from lots of different countries, that I would never have met if I didn't go gliding.'

So, next time you see a glider soaring overhead, it may well be Lyn flying her way to another badge or, knowing her love of the sport, just gliding for the sheer fun of it.

A After eight years' gliding experience, Lyn has achieved her Bronze and Silver Badges and is an Assistant Rated Instructor. She hopes to go on and earn more badges, as well as becoming a Full Rated Instructor in the future. Her role as an instructor provides her with some of gliding's most rewarding moments.

B To those of us on the ground gazing up, the pilot's skills are there for all to see, as the glider soars effortlessly on the warm air thermals. Lyn is not one to boast about her training though.

C But for all the achievement of solo flight, glider pilots have to work for one another, and this is another side of gliding that Lyn enjoys and appreciates.

D So with the first solo flight behind you, what's next?

E Lyn thinks for a moment when she's asked if she's ever had any emergencies to contend with.

F As a result, a friend of hers flew in a glider alongside her along the Innsbruck Valley at mountain top height ... that's around seven thousand, four hundred feet.

G To get the Silver, for example, you have to get over 1,000 m in height, complete a five-hour flight and then a 50 km flight to a designated airfield.

H As PA to our Managing Director, Lyn has to be pretty level-headed, but in her spare time, she likes nothing better than to have her head in the clouds, indulging in her passion for gliding.

PART 4

You are going to read some information about airports in Britain. For questions
22–35, *choose from the airports* (**A–H**). *Some of the airports may be chosen more*
than once. When more than one answer is required, these may be given in any
order. There is an example at the beginning (**0**).
Mark your answers **on the separate answer sheet**.

Which airport:

does not sell anything to read?	**0** *H*		
has shops which sell highly-priced goods?	**22**	**23**	
seems to have put its seating in the wrong place?	**24**		
makes it very easy for passengers to find their way through?	**25**		
has its shops spread out?	**26**		
has a departure lounge which is not very impressive?	**27**	**28**	
has a badly-situated café?	**29**		
changes its range of food according to the season?	**30**		
has an unexpectedly disappointing range of shops?	**31**		
has a good view of the planes?	**32**		
has facilities for people who are travelling for work?	**33**	**34**	
needs modernising?	**35**		

Which airport?

The choice of where to fly from has never been greater, particularly for those flying on a package holiday. For each airport, we looked at the facilities (e.g. restaurants, waiting areas, etc.) offered before going through passport control (land-side) and after going through passport control (air-side).

A   Heathrow 4

The check-in hall is spacious and modern. There are few land-side shops but the essentials are available. A café with pine seating and a medium range of hot dishes and salads is situated upstairs. There are more facilities air-side. The shops are clustered into the central part of the 500-metre long hall, and expensive ranges are well represented. There's plenty of natural light from the windows that overlook the runway and lots of seating away from the shopping area.

B   Manchester 2

The check-in hall has a high glass roof which lets in natural light. The café is at one end and slightly separated from the rest of the facilities, which makes it much more pleasant. There's also an up-market coffee shop. Hundreds of seats – little used when we visited despite the passengers crowded below – are available upstairs. The departure lounge is bright and has plenty of space, the cafeteria is pleasant.

C   Stansted

Passengers can walk in a straight line from the entrance, through the check-in to the monorail that takes them to their plane. Land-side, ⇒→

there's a cluster of fast food outlets that sell baked potatoes, American burgers and filled rolls. All seating is in the same area away from the check-in and shops. There's a surprisingly small number of shops considering Stansted's claims to be a major London airport, although basic stores like a chemist and bookshop are here. The large departure lounge has blue seats and grey carpet. There's a large tax-free and luxury goods shopping area and a café.

D   Heathrow 2

Avoid travelling from here if you can. The check-in area is unpleasant with a claustrophobic low roof and scores of pillars. The upstairs café is noisy because it is next to the music shop. The departure lounge is also too small with illuminated advertisements hanging from its low ceiling.

E   Manchester 1

The large, low check-in hall is the least impressive part of the terminal. Beyond that is a pleasant shopping mall with a wide range of shops and snack bars. The self-service eating area has a good range of foods from steak and chips to salads. There is also a more formal restaurant mostly used for business lunches. The departure lounge is large and bright.

F   Edinburgh

The eating options range from a coffee shop to a self-service restaurant, and a reasonable variety of shops are scattered around the land-side area rather than being collected in one area. The air-side food arrangements are mainly limited to rolls and buns.

G   East Midlands

The check-in area is in a long, low building where the roof is supported by a forest of pillars which interrupt the line of vision. There's a café and bar upstairs along with a pizza restaurant during the summer. The main eating area is downstairs and mainly serves sandwiches and cakes along with a hot dish of the day. The departure lounge is pleasant with natural light and plenty of dark blue seats. The Sherwood Lounge has easy chairs and sofas and is aimed at commercial travellers.

H   Cardiff

The facilities are simple and the decoration is showing its age. Shopping is extremely limited with only bare essentials available. There are no books or magazines for sale. The restaurant is unappealing. The tiny departure lounge is dark and uninviting.

PAPER 2 WRITING (1 hour 30 minutes)

PART 1

*You **must** answer this question.*

1   You are interested in attending a language course in England next summer. You have seen the advertisement below. You have also talked to your English teacher and she has suggested some things that you should check before you register.

Read the advertisement below, together with your teacher's note. Then write to the language school, asking for information about the points mentioned by your teacher, and anything else that you think is important.

SUMMER LANGUAGE COURSES

2 weeks, 3 weeks, 1 month

Beautiful English market town. Full sports and social programme. Accommodation with friendly English families. Helpful teachers. Small classes.

Full details from: Ian Lawrence, The Smart School of English, High Street, Little Bonnington

It's a great idea for you to do a language course in England. Be careful to choose a good school. When you write, ask about these things:
- student numbers, ages
- details of sports programme etc.
- local facilities
- teachers' qualifications
Let me know if you need any more help. Good luck!

Write **a letter** of between **120–180** words in an appropriate style on the next page. Do not write any addresses.

PART 1

....
....
....
....
....
....
....
....
....
....
....
....
....
....
....
....
....
....
....
....
....
....
....
....
....
....
....
....
....
....
....

PART 2

*Write an answer to **one** of the questions **2–5** in this part. Write your answer in* **120–180** *words in an appropriate style on the next page, putting the question number in the box.*

2   An international young people's magazine is investigating the question:
    Do young people today really know what they want from life?

    Write a short **article** for this magazine on this topic based on your own experience.

3   You have decided to enter this competition.

> # Exciting chance for writers!
>
> Write a short story and win a Great Prize
>
> Your entry must begin or end with the following words:
>
> *No matter what people said about Alex, I knew he was a true friend.*

    Write your **story** for the competition.

4   You are attending a summer language course and have been asked to report on a local leisure facility (e.g. cinema, sports hall, etc) for the benefit of students attending the next course.

    Write your **report** describing the facility and what it has to offer, and commenting on its good and bad points.

5   **Background reading texts**

    Answer **one** of the following two questions based on your reading of **one** of the set books (see p.2). Write the title of the book next to the question number box.

    Either **(a)** Describe your favourite character in the book and explain what you like about him/her.

    or **(b)** Explain how the physical setting of the book is important to the success of the story.

PART 2

Question	

....

....

....

....

....

....

....

....

....

....

....

....

....

....

....

....

....

....

....

....

....

....

....

....

....

....

....

....

....

....

....

PAPER 3 USE OF ENGLISH (1 hour 15 minutes)

For questions 1–15, read the text below and decide which answer A, B, C or D
best fits each space. There is an example at the beginning (0).
Mark your answers on the separate answer sheet.

Example:

0   **A** expect   **B** count   **C** claim   **D** prepare

0	A	B	C	D
	▬	▭	▭	▭

ACTION SCENES IN FILMS

Modern cinema audiences **(0)** .... to see plenty of thrilling scenes in action films.
These scenes, which are **(1)** .... as stunts, are usually **(2)** .... by stuntmen who are
specially trained to do dangerous things safely. **(3)** .... can crash a car, but if you're
shooting a film, you have to be extremely **(4)** .... , sometimes stopping **(5)** .... in front
of the camera and film crew. At an early **(6)** .... in the production, an expert
stuntman is **(7)** .... in to work out the action scenes and form a team. He is the only
person who can go **(8)** .... the wishes of the director, **(9)** .... he will usually only do
this in the **(10)** .... of safety.

Many famous actors like to do the dangerous parts themselves, which produces
better shots, since stuntmen don't have to **(11)** .... in for the actors. Actors like to
become **(12)** .... in all the important aspects of the character they are playing, but
without the recent progress in safety equipment, insurance companies would
never **(13)** .... them take the risk. To do their own stunts, actors need to be good
athletes, but they must also be sensible and know their **(14)** .... . If they were to be
hurt, the film would **(15)** .... to a sudden halt.

1   **A** remarked   **B** known   **C** referred   **D** named

2   **A** performed   **B** given   **C** fulfilled   **D** displayed

3   **A** Everyone   **B** Someone   **C** Anyone   **D** No-one

4   **A** detailed   **B** plain   **C** straight   **D** precise

5   **A** right   **B** exact   **C** direct   **D** strict

6   **A** period   **B** minute   **C** part   **D** stage

7   **A** led   **B** taken   **C** drawn   **D** called

8   **A** over   **B** against   **C** through   **D** across

9   **A** despite   **B** so   **C** although   **D** otherwise

10   **A** interests   **B** needs   **C** purposes   **D** regards

11   **A** work   **B** get   **C** put   **D** stand

12   **A** connected   **B** arranged   **C** involved   **D** affected

13   **A** allow   **B** let   **C** permit   **D** admit

14   **A** limits   **B** ends   **C** frontiers   **D** borders

15   **A** come   **B** fall   **C** pull   **D** go

PART 2

*For questions **16–30**, read the text below and think of the word which best fits each space. Use only **one** word in each space. There is an example at the beginning (**0**).*
*Write your word **on the separate answer sheet**.*

Example: | 0 | *or* | | 0 |
|---|---|---|---|
| | | | __ __ |

SHARKS

For anyone who wants either to film **(0)** .... study great white sharks, Australian expert, Rodney Fox, is the first contact. Fox knows exactly **(16)** .... the sharks will be at different times of the year; and can even predict **(17)** .... they will behave around blood, divers and other sharks. He understands them as well as **(18)** .... else alive. In fact, he's lucky to *be* alive; a 'great white' once **(19)** .... to bite him in half.

Three decades **(20)** .... this near-fatal attack, Fox still carries the physical scars, but feels **(21)** .... hate for his attacker. Instead he organises three or four trips **(22)** .... year to bring scientists and photographers to the kingdom of the great white shark. **(23)** .... main aim of these trips is to improve people's understanding of an animal **(24)** .... evil reputation has become an excuse for killing it.

Great white sharks are not as amusing as dolphins and seals, **(25)** .... their role in the ocean is critical. They kill off sick animals, helping to prevent the spread **(26)** .... disease and to maintain the balance in the ocean's food chains. Fox feels a responsibility to act **(27)** .... a guardian of great white sharks. **(28)** .... the scientists, film makers and photographers can communicate their sense of wonder **(29)** .... other people, he is confident that understanding **(30)** .... replace hatred.

For questions 31–40, complete the second sentence so that it has a similar meaning to the first sentence, using the word given. **Do not change the word given**. *You must use between two and five words, including the word given. There is an example at the beginning (0).*
Write **only** *the missing words* **on the separate answer sheet**.

Example:

0   I last saw him at my 21st birthday party.
    since

    I .... my 21st birthday party.

The gap can be filled by the words 'haven't seen him since' so you write:

0	*haven't seen him since*	0	0 1 2

---

31   'You've broken my radio, Frank!' said Jane.
    accused

    Jane .... her radio.

32   My car really needs to be repaired soon.
    must

    I really .... repaired soon.

33   Susan regrets not buying that house.
    wishes

    Susan .... that house.

34   I could never have succeeded without your help.
    you

    I could never have succeeded .... me.

35   I thought I might run out of cash, so I took my cheque-book with me.
    case

    I took my cheque-book with me .... out of cash.

36 Linda's plans for a picnic have been spoilt by the weather.
fallen

Linda's plans for a picnic .... because of the weather.

37 The bread was too stale to eat.
fresh

The bread .... to eat.

38 Perhaps Brian went home early.
may

Brian .... home early.

39 I can't possibly work in all this noise!
impossible

It .... work in all this noise!

40 The thief suddenly realised that the police were watching him.
watched

The thief suddenly realised that he .... by the police.

PART 4

For questions **41–55**, read the text below and look carefully at each line. Some of the lines are correct, and some have a word which should not be there. If a line is correct, put a tick (✓) by the number **on the separate answer sheet**. If a line has a word which should **not** be there, write the word **on the separate answer sheet**. There are two examples at the beginning (**0** and **00**).

Examples:

0	✓	0

00	*own*	0

WHY I DISLIKE COMPUTERS

0	Almost everyone says that computers are wonderful and that they are
00	changing our own lives for the better by making everything faster and
41	more reliable, but I'm not so much sure that this is the case.
42	The other day I was standing in a large department store until
43	waiting to pay for a couple of films for my camera when the assistant
44	announced that the computer which controlled the till it had stopped
45	working. I didn't think this was a big problem and I set myself off to
46	find another counter, but of course, all the machines are one part of
47	the same system. So there we were: a shop full of customers, money
48	at the ready, waiting to make our purchases, but it was quite clear that
49	none out of the assistants knew what to do. They weren't allowed to
50	take our money and give to customers a written receipt, because the
51	sales wouldn't then have been recorded on the computer system.
52	In the end, like with many other people, I left my shopping on the
53	counter and walked out. Don't you think so that's ridiculous? It would
54	never have happened before computers, and that, for me, is all the
55	problem: we are beginning to depend on these machines for so
	completely that we simply can't manage without them any more.

PART 5

*For questions **56–65**, read the text below. Use the word given in capitals at the end of each line to form a word that fits in the space in the same line. There is an example at the beginning **(0)**. Write your word **on the separate answer sheet**.*

Example:

0	*unusual*	0 __ __

CAMERON PARK

At first light, there is nothing **(0)** .... about the town of Cameron Park in California but, as the day begins and the town comes to **(56)** .... , you can't help **(57)** .... that, among the cars, there are light aeroplanes moving along the roads towards the airport.

USUAL
LIVE
NOTICE

When the town was **(58)** .... built, a small airport was included for the **(59)** .... of people flying in to look at the properties which were for **(60)** .... , but it soon became clear to the developers that this was an attraction in itself. The streets were **(61)** .... so that planes could use them, the mailboxes near the road were made **(62)** .... to avoid passing wings, and all the electricity cables were buried **(63)** .... .

ORIGIN
CONVENIENT
SELL
WIDE
SHORT
GROUND

Now, there is every **(64)** .... that the residents will have a private plane in their garage and use it with the same **(65)** .... other people enjoy with their cars.

LIKELY
FREE
likelyhood

PAPER 4   LISTENING (approximately 40 minutes)

PART 1

You will hear people talking in eight different situations.
For questions 1–8, choose the best answer A, B or C.

1   You are visiting a museum when you hear this man addressing a group of
.   people.
    Who is he?

    A   a security guard

    B   a tourist guide   [| 1]

    C   a museum guide

2   You're in a restaurant when you overhear one of the waiters talking.
    Who is he talking about?

    A   a colleague

    B   the manager   [| 2]

    C   a customer

3   You're waiting in a hospital corridor when you hear this woman talking.
    What does she say about her doctor?

    A   He's made a mistake.

    B   He's been unhelpful.   [| 3]

    C   He's been untruthful.

4   You are out shopping when you hear a shop assistant talking to a customer.
    What is she refusing to do?

    A   give him some money

    B   change a faulty item   [| 4]

    C   repair something

5 Listen to this woman introducing the next speaker at a conference.
Why has she been asked to introduce him?

A He is an old friend.

B He is a former student of hers.

C He is a colleague.

5

6 You are staying in a farmhouse when you hear your host on the telephone.
Who is he talking to?

A a supplier

B a customer

C an employee

6

7 You hear this critic talking on the radio.
What is she recommending?

A a film

B a book

C an exhibition

7

8 You are walking up the street when you hear this man talking to a woman at
her front door.
What does he want to do?

A interview her

B help her

C advise her

8

PART 2

You will hear a student called Bill talking about his holiday job.
*For questions **9–18**, complete the notes which summarise what he says. You will*
need to write a word or a short phrase in the box.

Reason for doing job:

	9

Building used to be a

	10

Good position because it's near

	11

Main alteration: owner has added

	12

Bill's favourite task:

	13

Owner is very careful about

	14

Attitude of male residents to staff:

	15

Problem with woman who
thought he was

	16

Other staff treated Bill as

	17

Bill is going back in order to

	18

PART 3

You will hear five different women talking about parties.
For questions 19–23, choose from the list A–F what they describe. Use the letters only once. There is one extra letter which you do not need to use.

A She regretted having gone.

B She was surprised she enjoyed it.

C She was embarrassed by her friends.

D She thought it was badly organised.

E She hadn't known what sort of event it was.

F She met someone who admired her.

Speaker 1		19
Speaker 2		20
Speaker 3		21
Speaker 4		22
Speaker 5		23

PART 4

You will hear a conversation between two teenagers, Nick and Sandra.
*For questions **24–30**, decide which statements are true or false and mark your*
*answers **T** for True or **F** for False.*

24   Sandra had to do some housework before coming out. | | 24 |

25   Sandra envies Nick. | | 25 |

26   Sandra is angry with her mother. | | 26 |

27   Sandra has failed her exams. | | 27 |

28   Nick sympathises with Sandra's mother. | | 28 |

29   Sandra has lost the tickets. | | 29 |

30   Nick will go to the next concert on his own. | | 30 |

PAPER 5   SPEAKING (approximately 15 minutes)

Part 1

You tell the examiner about yourself. The examiner may ask you questions such as: Where are you from? How do you usually spend your free time? What are your plans for the future? Your partner does the same.

Part 2

The examiner gives you two pictures to look at and asks you to talk about them for about a minute. Your partner does the same with two different pictures.

Part 3

The examiner gives you a photograph or drawing to look at with your partner. You are asked to solve a problem or come to a decision about something in the picture. For example, you might be asked to decide the best way to use some rooms in a language school. You discuss the problem together.

Part 4

You are asked more questions connected with your discussion in Part 3. For example, you might be asked to talk about the best ways of studying.

Practice Test 2

PAPER 1 READING (1 hour 15 minutes)

*You are going to read a magazine article about exercising in water. Choose from the list (**A–I**) the sentence which best summarises each part (**1–7**) of the article. There is one extra sentence which you do not need to use. There is an example at the beginning (**0**).*

Mark your answers **on the separate answer sheet.**

A	You are unlikely to cause yourself an injury in water.
B	It is not as easy as it looks.
C	Aqua fitness can do more than simply help heal injuries.
D	You can lose weight and enjoy yourself at the same time.
E	You can strengthen your heart and muscles by training every day.
F	Your body will adapt to exercising in water.
G	Don't worry about what you look like.
H	Exercise in water puts less pressure on the heart.
I	The idea of exercising in water is not new.

Making a SPLASH

0	*I*

The last thing many people expect to do in a swimming pool these days is swim. The latest fitness phenomenon to make a big splash at the local pool is aqua fitness. The properties of water have long been known to make it one of the safest and most effective media in which to exercise. Physiotherapists have used it for years and, even as far back as the Romans, the value of water for healing has been recognised.

1	

Today 'aqua fitness', as it is known, has seen exercising in the swimming pool progressing from merely being an activity for the recovery of an injury. Aqua fitness has become a valuable training aid even for professional athletes who use it to reduce the risk of overtraining. However, that's not to say that exercising in water isn't ideal for the rest of us too, from the young to the old, from the fit to those who do suffer from complaints such as arthritis.

2	

Exercising in water raises the heart rate less than land aerobics. Lydia Campbell, a fitness expert, says there are no conclusive studies on why it has a less drastic effect on your heart, but there are some factors that partly explain it. Lydia says, 'Water is supportive, as we all know, and with blood flowing more easily, there is less stress on the heart.'

3	

There are other benefits to working out in water such as the fact that your muscles are less likely to ache the following day, the water has a massaging effect on the body, and of course, there is always the possibility of getting a bit slimmer. It is generally thought that an aqua fitness workout can use from 450 to 700 calories an hour. And don't forget, water is fun – exercising to music in water is a unique experience!

4	

The reassuring element of exercising in water is that, apart from doing you good, it is relatively difficult to do anything that is going to harm you.

5	

As far as modesty is concerned, if you miss a step, carry a little more excess weight than you feel comfortable with or just feel embarrassed because you haven't exercised before, there is no need to be anxious as everything is hidden beneath the water level!

6	

Getting used to moving in water takes a little time because of the gravity changes on the body. Running in water will be easier if your body has lots of muscle, but don't worry about this not being the case, as the exercising in water will strengthen muscles anyway. Soon you will be able to move more strongly through the pool.

7	

Classes usually start with a warm-up aimed at stimulating and raising the body temperature. Using the properties of water in an aqua workout can create an effective training programme that might change some previous ideas about how easy exercising in water is. Try running in shallow knee-deep water. It's easy, but try running in thigh-deep water and things suddenly get more difficult – chest-deep water is even harder, as the water resistance increases.

PART 2

*You are going to read a newspaper article about a television presenter called Sue Barker. For questions **8–15**, choose the answer (**A**, **B**, **C** or **D**) which you think fits best according to the text.*

*Mark your answers **on the separate answer sheet.***

SUE BARKER, the former tennis star, is to present the BBC TV Sports Programme *Grandstand* this summer. The BBC will shortly announce her promotion to one of television's top sports posts, confirming a rise in the media ranks that has been almost as rapid as her progress up the ladder of international tennis in the 1970s.

It is a remarkable comeback to national fame for a woman originally known for being the girlfriend of a pop star and for being a British player who won the French Open tennis tournament.

Her new media career is already very successful. It had a sudden beginning. A succession of injuries and a fall in her ranking from 16th to 63rd caused her to announce her retirement from the game in a dramatic on-court speech at the Australian Open tournament in 1984.

'I took the car back to my hotel where a message was waiting for me to ring a TV station in Sydney. I thought, "Oh God, not another interview", but they asked me to come and start on their sports programme the next day to give expert comment. There was no training, nothing.'

There was no training either when David Hill, then head of sport on Sky TV, recruited her two years ago to be one of the presenters on its Saturday sports programme.

'I turned up and was told my first broadcast was in a few minutes' time. It was a classic, absolutely awful. I rattled through it, it wasn't even making sense, and then I was left for the last four seconds just smiling at the camera.

'It was the longest four seconds of my life. Afterwards I said I wanted to give up, but David said, "You've only made two mistakes, I never sack anyone until they've made three". So I carried on doing five-minute slots – the sports news round-ups – which proved to be very good on-the-job training. Then came the approach from the BBC.'

While Sky took a quiet pride in the fact that the BBC wanted to sign up its star, its annoyance at losing Barker was understandable. It had allowed the BBC to have her for the tennis season and offered a half-and-half arrangement when the BBC wanted to sign her full-time – but the BBC was not interested. Sam Chisholm, Sky's chief executive, decided to take legal action.

In the BBC's tennis team, the strengths of Sue Barker were immediately obvious. She offered a number of technical insights, not just into the game but into the players' mental state, and was not afraid to be critical of those on the court who are still friends, a rare quality among the large number of former sports stars that fill the BBC commentary boxes.

For Barker, being a critic was not always easy, especially as she mixed socially with the players. They did sometimes get upset about it. 'Martina Navratilova watches everything, absolutely everything, and she came up to me quite angry one day, saying "I heard you, I heard what you said about Steffi Graf". But I will tell them exactly why I thought they weren't playing well, compare their performance with a previous one and, if they can honestly say to me they did play well, then I will apologise.'

Having been angry at some of the criticism of *her* during her 13 years of playing international tennis, she feels she can turn that knowledge to good use. 'I know what hurts and what doesn't hurt, and athletes tend to trust other athletes.'

8   What does the writer say about Sue Barker's career?
    A   She took a long time to become famous as a tennis star.
    B   She is better known as a TV presenter than a tennis star.
    C   She obtained an important TV job after a short time.
    D   She has tried a career in pop music.

9   What does 'it' in line 10 refer to?
    A   her tennis career
    B   her comeback
    C   her success on TV
    D   her fame

10 She became a sports commentator because
    A   she was advised to do so by tennis experts.
    B   an Australian TV channel suggested it.
    C   she decided she would prefer it to tennis.
    D   she was tired of being interviewed by other people.

11 What happened when she presented a Saturday sports programme?
    A   She made a better impression than she expected.
    B   The TV company liked the way she smiled at the camera.
    C   She talked for too long and too fast.
    D   The boss wasn't sure whether to sack her or not.

12 How did Sky TV feel when the BBC employed her?
    A   They turned down the offer to share her.
    B   They were glad for her sake.
    C   They did not want to lose her.
    D   They had expected this to happen.

13 How is she different from other sports commentators?
    A   She still has a lot of friends in the game.
    B   She has very good technical background.
    C   She finds it difficult to praise the players.
    D   She speaks the truth about friends.

14 What does she feel she can offer as a sports commentator?
    A   She can give athletes advice on dealing with the camera.
    B   She can make comments which athletes accept.
    C   She can help athletes to get on with each other.
    D   She can attract new viewers to sports programmes.

15 This article was written about Sue Barker because
    A   she is going to be in the public view a lot.
    B   there is a court case between Sky TV and the BBC.
    C   she has recently given up tennis.
    D   a well-known tennis star was recently upset by her.

*You are going to read a newspaper article about an artist. Seven paragraphs have been removed from the article. Choose from the paragraphs (**A–H**) the one which fits each gap (**16–21**). There is one extra paragraph which you do not need to use. There is an example at the beginning (**0**).*
*Mark your answers **on the separate answer sheet**.*

The life of Georgia O'Keeffe

Georgia O'Keeffe was born in 1887 and grew up in Sun Prairie, Wisconsin, a farming town settled only 40 years earlier.

0	*H*

When she was 16, her family moved to Virginia, and O'Keeffe studied art at the Art Institute of Chicago. At 23, she had a crisis of confidence and spoke of giving up painting, but over the next two years she taught art in Texas and in South Carolina, and eventually regained her desire to paint.

16	

O'Keeffe lived and studied in New York on and off for three years, taking time off to teach in Virginia, South Carolina and again in Texas. Always independent-minded, in Texas she became known for her strange clothes.

17	

A friend showed O'Keeffe's drawings to Alfred Stieglitz, the greatest photographer in America and owner of the forward-looking 291 Gallery in New York. When he unwrapped O'Keeffe's charcoal drawings, he was amazed. 'I realised that I had never seen anything like it before.'

18	

A year later, O'Keeffe gave up her teaching and started painting full-time in Manhattan, Maine and at the Stieglitz family home in Lake George, New York. She also joined Stieglitz's circle of friends, which included some of the most important writers, painters and photographers in America.

19	

While her work grew in confidence, her life with Stieglitz was full of difficulties. He encouraged her work but wanted her to be an obedient wife. In his role as her dealer he sought dictatorial control over the sale and exhibition of her work. O'Keeffe felt imprisoned by her marriage, genuinely loving though it was.

20	

And it gave rise to some of her greatest paintings: landscapes, studies of architecture, and still-lifes. In still-life she became obsessed with the animal skeletons she had collected in the desert.

21	

When Georgia O'Keeffe died, she was a year short of her century. Relatives gave some of O'Keeffe's work to American museums. They show the courage and persistence of one of the most remarkable of all women painters.

A During this period, O'Keeffe made a series of charcoal studies which she called her 'Special' drawings. These were the first work of her artistic maturity. And they were to lead to her first great romantic involvement.

B After Stieglitz died, O'Keeffe rarely visited the East Coast, and the life she led in New Mexico was increasingly solitary. She continued to work, though with decreasing energy (she was now 60 years old). Her work grew steadily in value and she became a very rich woman.

C Stieglitz exhibited the drawings without O'Keeffe's knowledge. Though initially outraged, she knew that 291 was the best possible venue for her work – and Stieglitz himself the best possible dealer. With time, he became equally passionate about O'Keeffe herself. She was 30 and Stieglitz was 53. In 1924 they married.

D She found her escape in New Mexico. She had long preferred the empty landscapes of the American West to the greenery of the East Coast. Even though she remained devoted to the ageing Stieglitz and spent winters with him in New York, New Mexico was her home for the rest of her life.

E The role did not entirely suit her. Solitary by nature and the only woman artist in a group of opinionated men, she was very aware of the oppression of women. Some of the men resented her, feeling threatened by a woman of such exceptional talent.

F O'Keeffe denied the connection and late in life she abruptly finished an interview when asked about it. She also painted New York's cityscape as well as rural architecture.

G O'Keeffe did not feel that her future lay in teaching, but then as now there were few other ways for an artist to earn a living. So she decided to take a teaching degree in New York, and her life was changed forever.

H O'Keeffe was drawn towards art from an early age. She was brilliant at drawing and, at 13, told a friend, 'I'm going to be an artist'.

PART 4

You are going to read a magazine article about New York cafés. For questions
22–34, *choose from the cafés* (**A–H**). *Some of the cafés may be chosen more than*
once. When more than one answer is required, these may be given in any order.
There is an example at the beginning (**0**).
For question **35**, *choose the answer* (**A, B, C** *or* **D**) *which you think fits best*
according to the text.
Mark your answers **on the separate answer sheet**.

Which of the cafés:

is close to a theatre?	**0**	*H*
does not have very interesting food?	**22**	
is near a well-known monument?	**23**	
is floating?	**24**	
offers some dishes for the health-conscious?	**25**	
is good for sitting and watching others?	**26**	**27**
appeals particularly to tourists?	**28**	
may offer you the chance of some physical exercise?	**29**	
is known by few people?	**30**	
is fairly cheap?	**31**	
has exciting American food?	**32**	
is good for a special evening out?	**33**	**34**

35 The purpose of the text is to
  A identify the liveliest outdoor café in New York.
  B identify the outdoor café in New York with the best food.
  C offer information about a range of eating opportunities in New York.
  D offer information about the eating habits of people in New York.

Big Apple al fresco

Scattered throughout the city of New York are dozens of 'secret' gardens, quiet corners, terraces and rooftops where you can escape the urban rush and dine amidst trees and flowering plants.

A   TAVERN ON THE GREEN

Some call it a tourist trap, but the architecture and woodland setting guarantee a long and healthy life for this Central Park restaurant. Dinner in the garden on a summer's night, wrapped in the scent of a thousand flowers and lit by Japanese lanterns, is truly an affair to remember. And the extravagant desserts are a luscious way to celebrate a birthday or other special occasion.

B   BOATHOUSE CAFÉ

While tourists are queuing up for tables at Tavern on the Green, New Yorkers head deeper into Central Park for lunch at this charming, relatively inexpensive café. The main attraction here is the setting, which overlooks the park's Boathouse Pond with the skyscrapers of midtown in the ⟫→

background. The food at the Boathouse is admittedly unimpressive although you won't go wrong with the pasta dishes or burgers.

C COURTYARD CAFÉ & BAR

Located in the heart of midtown near Grand Central Terminal, this eatery in the Doral Court Hotel qualifies as one of New York's best-kept secrets. The garden here, though small, is one of the city's finest with umbrella-shaded tables next to a sparkling waterfall.

D AMERICAN FESTIVAL CAFÉ

'Golden Boy', the famous statue, oversees the festivities at this restaurant situated in the shadow of New York's Art Deco architectural masterpiece. In winter, the outdoor section of the café is transformed into the Rockefeller Center Skating Rink; in summer, the shaded, linen-draped tables make an inviting prospect after a hard morning of shopping.

E RIVER CAFÉ

New York City's best outdoor dining experience is across the Brooklyn Bridge at this boat-restaurant moored in the East River. In an informal survey, six out of seven New Yorkers picked the River Café as the best place in the city to propose marriage. Positive features: stunning views of the Manhattan skyline, and of picture-perfect sunsets; inventive contemporary cooking with an American accent.

F MANHATTAN CHILLI COMPANY

Outdoor cafés are thick on the ground in Greenwich Village – it's hardly worth recommending one, since visitors so quickly find their own. It's easy to walk by the Manhattan Chilli Company which looks like just another quaint Village restaurant from the street. Step inside, though, and you'll discover gigantic bowls of good chilli served in a peaceful garden.

G YAFFA CAFÉ

When the western half of Greenwich Village changed into a center for tourists, the area's artists and musicians moved east to the neighbourhood known as Alphabet City. For a glimpse of arty New York, 1990s style, take a seat in Yaffa's uniquely urban garden; order a plate of food and a pot of herb tea and watch the world go by.

H JOSEPHINA

An excellent position across the street from Lincoln Center for the Performing Arts draws diners to this exotic restaurant; the delicately seasoned recipes and fresher-than-fresh ingredients bring them back. Owner/chef Louis Lanza uses flavoured oils and fresh stocks to delight the taste-buds without excessive sugar or fat. (The exception: sinfully rich desserts. Shrugs Lanza, 'Nobody's perfect.') Josephina offers two outdoor options, a sidewalk café that's perfect for people-watching and a lushly landscaped back garden.

PAPER 2 WRITING (1 hour 30 minutes)

PART 1

*You **must** answer this question.*

1   Your friend has seen this job advertisement and is planning to apply. You
    worked for the same company last year. Using the information in the
    advertisement and the notes you have made on it, tell your friend what the job
    was really like and give him or her any advice you think necessary.

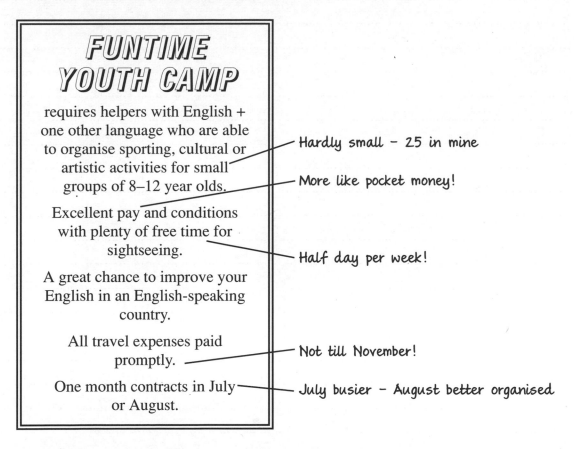

Write **a letter** of between **120–180** words in an appropriate style on the next
page. Do not write any addresses.

PART 1

PART 2

*Write an answer to **one** of the questions **2–5** in this part. Write your answer in **120–180** words in an appropriate style on the next page, putting the question number in the box.*

2   Your school magazine or company newsletter has decided to use its back page for a regular entertainment section. Write a **review** of a film or play you have seen recently, describing the film or play and saying why you would or would not recommend others to go and see it.

3   You see this notice in a magazine for learners of English, and decide to send in a story:

> We wish to publish a collection of stories from our readers, all with the title **The day that did most for my English**.
>
> If you have an interesting or amusing story which you would like to share with others, please send it to us as soon as possible.

Write your **story** for the magazine.

4   Your teacher has asked you to describe some of the ways in which the place where you live has changed during your lifetime. Write a **description**, explaining whether these changes are for the better or the worse, and why you think this.

5   **Background reading texts**

Answer **one** of the following two questions based on your reading of **one** of the set books (see p.2). Write the title of the book next to the question number box.

Either   **(a)** Describe any character or event in the book which you find improbable and explain why.

or   **(b)** Describe the opening of the book and say whether it made you want to read the rest of the story. Explain why or why not.

PART 2

Question	

....
....
....
....
....
....
....
....
....
....
....
....
....
....
....
....
....
....
....
....
....
....
....
....
....
....
....

PAPER 3   USE OF ENGLISH (1 hour 15 minutes)

*For questions 1–15, read the text below and decide which answer **A, B, C** or **D**
best fits each space. There is an example at the beginning (**0**).
Mark your answers **on the separate answer sheet**.*

Example:
0   A in   **B** along   **C** up   **D** over

0	A	B	C	D
	—			

A VISITOR FOR MISS DREDGER

Every summer Miss Dredger took (**0**) .... visitors at Clôs de Joi. It was a square
house with a (**1**) .... across the island to the sea, with the island of Jersey on the
(**2**) .... .

Miss Dredger had (**3**) .... a carriage to take her down the harbour hill. (**4**) .... it was a
steep descent, she would (**5**) .... have taken it in her purposeful stride, and would
even have returned (**6**) .... foot up the long slope, for Miss Dredger scorned all
physical (**7**) .... .

Nevertheless, she had (**8**) .... on a carriage this (**9**) .... morning, for she had a
gentleman to meet at the harbour. Both he and his luggage must be got up the
harbour hill. It was (**10**) .... that the luggage could not walk up on its own and from
what she knew about men, it was ten (**11**) .... one that her new lodger (**12**) .... be as
helpless as his luggage.

And so, as the carriage had to go down the hill before it could come up again, Miss
Dredger, with her sharp (**13**) .... of logic, decided that, in order to (**14**) .... use of this
fact, it would be as well to be (**15**) .... for at Clôs de Joi.

1 **A** sight   **B** vision   **C** view   **D** look

2 **A** distance   **B** background   **C** outskirts   **D** horizon

3 **A** ordered   **B** required   **C** commanded   **D** asked

4 **A** However   **B** Although   **C** Despite   **D** Even

5 **A** commonly   **B** actually   **C** mostly   **D** normally

6 **A** at   **B** on   **C** with   **D** off

7 **A** weakness   **B** lightness   **C** tenderness   **D** softness

8 **A** decided   **B** chosen   **C** arranged   **D** considered

9 **A** definite   **B** certain   **C** particular   **D** individual

10 **A** honest   **B** simple   **C** direct   **D** plain

11 **A** to   **B** by   **C** for   **D** under

12 **A** should   **B** would   **C** ought   **D** could

13 **A** sense   **B** idea   **C** feeling   **D** impression

14 **A** take   **B** have   **C** make   **D** get

15 **A** looked   **B** visited   **C** sent   **D** called

PART 2

For questions **16–30**, *read the text below and think of the word which best fits each space. Use only* **one** *word in each space. There is an example at the beginning* **(0)**.
Write your word **on the separate answer sheet**.

Example: | 0 | *one* | 0 |

THE HORSE IN ART

There is little doubt that **(0)** .... of the chief roles of the horse in art, just **(16)** .... in life, is that of our servant and companion. We can have very little idea of **(17)** .... a horse feels in its natural state. Left to itself, **(18)** .... is unlikely that it would pull a plough, take a soldier **(19)** .... a dangerous situation in battle, **(20)** .... do most of the other things that have attracted painters and writers to the animal ever **(21)** .... the dawn of history.

The horse is controlled **(22)** .... the wishes of its owner. When we describe it, we say it has **(23)** .... virtues and qualities we most admire in ourselves and it is as the symbol **(24)** .... these qualities that it has so often **(25)** .... praised by painters and poets. Then we must consider the horse's own beauty, speed and strength. **(26)** .... truth, the picture we **(27)** .... most frequently moved by, in both art and literature, is actually a single image that combines all the advantages of the animal and its rider. An outstanding example of **(28)** .... is provided by the school of sculpture and painting in **(29)** .... the authority and personality of individuals is emphasised by the **(30)** .... that they are on horseback.

PART 3

*For questions **31–40**, complete the second sentence so that it has a similar meaning to the first sentence, using the word given.* **Do not change the word given.** *You must use between two and five words, including the word given. There is an example at the beginning (**0**).*
*Write **only** the missing words **on the separate answer sheet**.*

Example:

0   I last saw him at my 21st birthday party.
      since

      I .... my 21st birthday party.

The gap can be filled by the words 'haven't seen him since' so you write:

0	*haven't seen him since*	0	0 1 2

---

31   Do you know who this coat belongs to?
       coat

       Do you know .... is?

32   Jo's training accident meant she couldn't take part in the race.
       prevented

       Jo's training accident .... part in the race.

33   Cyclists are not allowed to ride on the station platform.
       must

       Bicycles .... on the station platform.

34   To Alan's amazement, the passport office was closed when he arrived.
       find

       Alan .... the passport office closed when he arrived.

35   It isn't necessary to book tickets for the show in advance.
       need

       You .... tickets for the show in advance.

36 The top shelf was so high that the children couldn't reach it.
high

The top shelf was .... the children to reach.

37 I'd prefer you to start work next week.
rather

I .... work next week.

38 'Do you remember what you have to do?' the teacher asked her class.
what

The teacher asked her class if .... to do.

39 It's unusual for Carol to get angry with her staff.
hardly

Carol .... temper with her staff.

40 There is no ice-cream left.
run

We .... ice-cream.

PART 4

For questions **41–55**, read the text below and look carefully at each line. Some of the lines are correct, and some have a word which should not be there. If a line is correct, put a tick (✓) by the number **on the separate answer sheet**. If a line has a word which should **not** be there, write the word **on the separate answer sheet**. There are two examples at the beginning (**0** and **00**).

Examples:

0	✓	0
00	*as*	0

A LETTER OF APOLOGY

Dear Richard,

0	Thanks very much for your letter. It was good to hear
00	all your news and I'm glad that your family are all as well.
41	It's very kind of you to invite for me to stay with you in
42	the June, but unfortunately my final exams are that month
43	and I don't yet know of the dates. I think they may be in
44	the week that you've suggested. In any case, judging
45	from my last Geography results, I will need to be studying
46	rather more than having a good time with my friends.
47	As soon as I will get the dates, I'll let you know but I
48	don't much expect I'll be able to come. Perhaps we'll be
49	able to get something organised for July. It's a long time
50	ever since we got together and I'd love to catch up on
51	what has been happening to you. If only your parents
52	don't want their house full of visitors in the holiday, you
53	could come over to stay with me. There's a plenty of
54	room and the house is just at a short bike ride from the
55	beach, so there would be lots to do. Let me know it if you

think this is a good idea.

Best wishes

For questions **56–65**, read the text below. Use the word given in capitals at the end of each line to form a word that fits in the space in the same line. There is an example at the beginning (**0**). Write your word **on the separate answer sheet**.

Example: | 0 | *natural* | 0 |

AN IMPORTANT ENGLISH TOWN

The site of the town of Winchester was a **(0)** .... place for a | **NATURE**
(56) .... , at the point where a river cut through the chalk of the | **SETTLE**
(57) .... hillsides. A simple camp at St Catherine's Hill was the | **SOUTH**
(58) .... known use of the site. This was followed by an Iron Age | **EARLY**
hill-fort, but this was left **(59)** .... by 100 BC. It was the Romans who | **INHABIT**
finally established the town and **(60)** .... it with a defensive wall for | **ROUND**
the protection of their people and trade.

With the **(61)** .... of its first cathedral in the seventh century, the | **BUILD**
town became an important **(62)** .... centre. Later, King Alfred, who | **RELIGION**
had **(63)** .... pushed back the invading Danes, moved his palace | **SUCCESS**
to Winchester. The town then experienced rapid **(64)** .... , and | **DEVELOP**
its **(65)** .... role in English history was underlined in 1066 when the | **CENTRE**
conquering Normans, like Alfred, made Winchester their capital.

PAPER 4   LISTENING (approximately 40 minutes)

PART 1

You will hear people talking in eight different situations.
For questions 1–8, choose the best answer, A, B or C.

1   You are walking round a market when you hear this woman talking to a customer.
    What is she doing?

    A   asking the customer's opinion

    B   offering a cheap sample

    C   explaining a price rise

2   You're in the doctor's waiting room when you overhear the nurse on the phone.
    Why didn't she send off the notes?

    A   She didn't know they were wanted.

    B   It isn't part of her job to do it.

    C   She didn't know which notes to send.

3   You're in a gallery when you hear these women talking.
    What are they looking at?

    A   a bowl

    B   a lamp

    C   a vase

4   You are visiting a large company and you hear two people talking.
    What are they discussing?

    A   a personal computer

    B   a typewriter

    C   a CD player

5 Listen to this clerk at a station booking office.
Which is the cheapest ticket?

    A a period return

    B an ordinary return

    C a Rover

	5

6 These friends are talking about a film.
Who will go to see it?

    A both of them

    B neither of them

    C the girl

	6

7 These people are talking about a colleague.
What's his problem?

    A His boss is unfair to him.

    B He has been ill.

    C He has too much to do.

	7

8 Listen to this woman phoning a travel agent.
What does she want to do?

    A cancel her booking

    B postpone her holiday

    C change her destination

	8

PART 2

You will hear an interview about sports facilities.
For questions 9–18, fill in the answers on the questionnaire.

Where does the interviewee live? **9**

What is the interviewee's occupation? **10**

How often does s/he use a public swimming pool? **11**

What does s/he feel about the opening times? **12**

What about entry charges? **13**

What does s/he feel about existing facilities? **14**

What would s/he most like to see added to these? **15**

What other sports should be catered for locally? **16**

Where should money for improvements come from? **17**

Who should be able to use the pool free? **18**

PART 3

You will hear five people talking to someone they have just met.
*For questions **19–23**, choose which of the people **A–F** each speaker is talking to.*
Use the letters only once. There is one extra letter which you do not need to use.

A a tenant

B a neighbour

C a holidaymaker

D a colleague at work

E a trainee

F a hotel guest

Speaker 1	19
Speaker 2	20
Speaker 3	21
Speaker 4	22
Speaker 5	23

PART 4

You will hear a discussion between Andy and Sharon about advertising their small business.
*For questions **24–30**, decide which of the statements are true and which are false and write **T** for True or **F** for False in the box provided.*

24 They have decided to spend some money on advertising. | 24

25 Their customers found their last advertisement boring. | 25

26 They need to attract better staff. | 26

27 Andy has contacted the local newspaper. | 27

28 They agree to advertise once a week. | 28

29 Sharon thinks a professional delivery company would cost too much. | 29

30 Andy agrees they should employ students. | 30

PAPER 5 SPEAKING (approximately 15 minutes)

Part 1

You tell the examiner about yourself. The examiner may ask you questions such as: Where are you from? How do you usually spend your free time? What are your plans for the future? Your partner does the same.

Part 2

The examiner gives you two pictures to look at and asks you to talk about them for about a minute. Your partner does the same with two different pictures.

Part 3

The examiner gives you a photograph or drawing to look at with your partner. You are asked to solve a problem or come to a decision about something in the picture. For example, you might be asked to decide the best way to use some rooms in a language school. You discuss the problem together.

Part 4

You are asked more questions connected with your discussion in Part 3. For example, you might be asked to talk about the best ways of studying.

Practice Test 3

PART 1

*You are going to read a newspaper article about women and technical subjects. Choose from the list (**A–I**) the sentence which best summarises each part (**1–7**) of the article. There is one extra sentence which you do not need to use. There is an example at the beginning (**0**).*
*Mark your answers **on the separate answer sheet**.*

A	Women often can't find, or don't think of looking for, the opportunities they need.
B	Women are needed in jobs that require a technological background.
C	Women study basic subjects alongside more specialised ones.
D	At the end of the course, women usually find jobs in local industry.
E	Women who want to change their jobs cannot because they have the wrong qualifications.
F	It is difficult to convince women and girls that they should take up scientific subjects.
G	In one training centre, the women are very eager to study scientific and technological subjects.
H	It is often difficult to obtain a place on a course.
I	My early interests were not developed.

Visual materials for Paper 5

1A

1B

2A

2B

1C

1D

2C

2D

1E

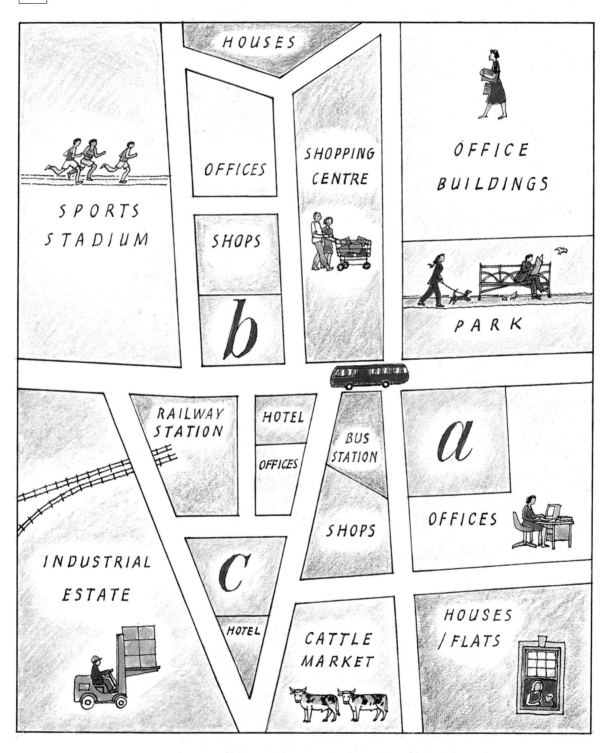

2E

Gifts for all!

2F

Miguel

Julia

Tom

Helen

4E

3A

3B

4A

4B

3C

3D

4C

4D

Success in sport

talent
unlimited money
lots of practice
sympathetic family
good equipment/facilities
professional coaching

Workface

A second chance to pick up a screwdriver, plug into the future and join the enthusiasts back at school

0	*I*

'I'VE always been interested in electronics and I often opened up the TV or the hi-fi to have a look. But I wasn't encouraged at school; I was the only girl in the Physics class and I felt lonely and depressed.'

1	

Susan Veerasamie's experience is typical of many. Eager to be the same as their friends, teenage girls shy away from technical and science subjects at school and then after a few years in a low-paid dead-end, 'woman's' job, they find they haven't got the qualifications to enable them to change course.

2	

The Haringey Women's Training and Education Centre, which Susan Veerasamie attends, is one of a handful of centres offering women a second chance to study technological and engineering subjects. It is housed in part of a former secondary school in north London and I doubt that the building has ever seen such keen students.

3	

The Centre provides courses in electronics, computing, the construction trades and science and technical skills, and everyone attends classes in numeracy, English and business practice.

4	

Hopefully, when they have completed their courses, the Centre's students will have gained enough confidence and basic skills to find a job or go on to further study. Nevertheless, getting on to a course at a college of further education is not easy if you don't have the required qualifications. The Manpower Services Commission offers courses in craft and technological skills which are open to everyone who is unemployed. However, places are often in high demand and the courses offered depend on the needs of local industry.

5	

There are other introductory and 'taster' courses similar to the Haringey Centre's around the country but they are scarce. It is often difficult for women to find a course that meets their needs and there is little to attract the attention of those who may never have considered work in the engineering and technological fields.

6	

The problem is how to persuade girls to broaden their options, and also to introduce training and retraining to women who have chosen more traditional paths, only to find the way to improved employment prospects closed or, at best, unsatisfying.

7	

Encouraging women to enter traditional 'male' work areas in greater numbers in this way is not only important for the women themselves, in that it offers a route into higher paid work, but it is also important for the country as a whole. There is a general skills shortage in the technological industries. We need these women's enthusiasm and ability.

PART 2

*You are going to read an extract about children's fiction. For questions **8–15**, choose the answer (**A, B, C** or **D**) which you think fits best according to the text.*
*Mark your answers **on the separate answer sheet**.*

What is good writing for children?

The children's publishers will tell you they look for 'good writing'. What exactly do they mean?

Before you send a story you have written to any publisher at all, your severest critic ought to be you yourself. To have a chance of succeeding in the competitive market of children's fiction, you should constantly be aware, every single time you sit down at your word-processor, of the need to produce 'good, original writing'. A difficult task, maybe, but one which hopefully we will help you to achieve.

To begin with, let us try to pin down exactly what publishers mean when they talk about 'good writing' for children. A useful starting point would be to take a look at some of the children's books which won literary prizes last year. Reading these books is one of the easiest and most enjoyable ways of: (a) finding out what individual publishers are publishing at the moment, and (b) learning a few tricks of the trade from well-established professionals. It goes without saying, of course, that slavishly copying the style and subject matter of a successful author is usually a recipe for disaster. Nor should you become downhearted after reading a particularly brilliant piece of work, and miserably think you will never be able to match up to those standards. Remember, overnight success is rare – most successful children's authors will have struggled long and hard to learn their trade. Read these books as a critic; note down the things you enjoyed or admired, as well as areas where you feel there was possibly room for improvement. After all, nobody is perfect, not even a successful, prize-winning author.

Possibly the toughest challenge is right at the youngest end of the age range – the picture book. The would-be author/illustrator is attempting to create an exciting story out of the narrow, limited, everyday world of a young child's experience – not easy at all. The whole storyline has to be strong enough to keep the reader turning the pages, yet simple enough to fit into a few pages. Another problem for the new picture-book author is that it can seem that every subject and every approach has been done to death, with nothing new left to say. Add to this the fact that printing costs are high because of full colour illustrations, which means that the publisher will probably want a text that suits the international market to increase sales, and a novel for ten-year olds, with hardly any pictures at all, starts to look much more inviting.

You would be forgiven for wondering if there are any truly original plots left to impress publishers with. But remember that, in many ways, it is the writer's own personal style, and intelligent handling of a subject that can change a familiar, overworked plot into something original and fresh. To illustrate this, read *The Enchanted Horse* by Magdalen Nabb. A young girl called Irina finds an old wooden horse in a junk shop, takes it home and treats it as if it was real. Soon it magically starts to come to life ... Sounds familiar? The magic object that comes alive is a storyline that has been used in hundreds of other children's stories. So why does it succeed here? The answer is that Magdalen Nabb has created a strong, believable character in the lonely, unhappy heroine Irina, and the descriptions of her relationship with the wooden horse are poetic and touching.

So, to return to the question asked at the beginning: What exactly is 'good writing' for children? The answer is that it is writing which is fresh, exciting and unpredictable, and which gives a new and original angle on what might be a well-worn subject. But do not be put off if you feel that you simply cannot match up to all these requirements. While there is obviously no substitute for talent, and the ability to come up with suitable ideas, many of the techniques for improving and polishing your manuscript can be learned.

8 Why does the article advise people to look at prize-winning books?
   A to copy the author's style
   B to realise what a high standard needs to be reached
   C to get an idea of what might be successful
   D to find out how to trick publishers

9 What do most successful children's authors have in common?
   A They did not get depressed by early failures.
   B They have learned how to be critical of other authors' work.
   C They find it easy to think of storylines that will sell.
   D They have worked hard to become well-known.

10 Why is the picture book the most difficult to write?
   A There is a limited range of subjects available.
   B Young children cannot follow storylines easily.
   C The pictures need to be exciting.
   D Children want to be able to read it quickly.

11 What looks 'more inviting' in line 54?
   A the international market
   B the increased sales
   C the novel for ten-year-olds
   D the type of pictures

12 The book about Irina is successful
   A because of the unusual way magic is used.
   B because of the way the character is described.
   C because the story has not been told before.
   D because the pictures bring the story to life.

13 What does 'it' refer to in line 68?
   A the storyline
   B the magic object
   C the horse
   D the children's story

14 What conclusion does the writer of the text come to?
   A Anyone can learn to write a good story.
   B The subject matter is the most important consideration.
   C If you have natural ability, you can learn the rest.
   D Some published fiction is badly written.

15 Why was this text written?
   A to explain what kind of books children like to read
   B to give advice to people who want to write children's fiction
   C to discourage new authors from being too optimistic
   D to persuade new authors to get away from old ideas

*You are going to read a magazine article about bodyclocks. Seven sentences have been removed from the article. Choose from the sentences (**A–H**) the one which fits each gap (**16–21**). There is one extra sentence which you do not need to use. There is an example at the beginning (**0**).*
*Mark your answers **on the separate answer sheet**.*

RHYTHM OF LIFE

Scientists have discovered that our bodies operate on a 25-hour day. So tuning into your bodyclock can make things really tick, says Jenny Hope, *Daily Mail* Medical Correspondent.

Choosing the right time to sleep, the correct moment to make decisions, the best hour to eat – and even go into hospital – could be your key to perfect health.

Centuries after man discovered the rhythms of the planets and the cycles of crops, scientists have learned that we too live by precise rhythms that govern the ebb and flow of everything from our basic bodily functions to mental skills. **0** *H.*

But it's not just the experts who are switching on to the way our bodies work. **16** Prince Charles consults a chart which tells him when he will be at his peak on a physical, emotional and intellectual level. Boxer Frank Bruno is another who charts his bio-rhythms to plan for big fights.

17 Sleep, blood pressure, hormone levels and heartbeat all follow their own clocks, which may bear only slight relation to our man-made 24-hour cycle.

Research shows that in laboratory experiments when social signals and, most crucially, light indicators such as dawn are taken away, people lose touch with the 24-hour clock and sleeping patterns change. **18**

In the real world, light and dark keep adjusting internal clocks to the 24-hour day. **19** As it falls from a 10 p.m. high of 37.2°C to a pre-dawn low of 36.1°C, mental functions fall too. This is a key reason why shift work can cause so many problems – both for workers and their organisations.

20 The three operators in the control room worked alternating weeks of day, evening and night shifts – a dangerous combination which never gave their bodies' natural rhythms a chance to settle down. Investigators believe this caused the workers to over-look a warning light and fail to close an open valve.

Finding the secret of what makes us tick has long fascinated scientists and work done over the last decade has yielded important clues.

21 [ ] For example, the time we eat may be important if we want to maximise intellectual or sporting performance. There is already evidence suggesting that the time when medicine is given to patients affects how well it works.

A Temperature and heartbeat cycles lengthen and settle into 'days' lasting about 25 hours.

B The most famous example is the nuclear accident at Three Mile Island in the US.

C But the best indicator of performance is body temperature.

D Leading experts say every aspect of human biology is influenced by daily rhythms.

E Dr Michael Stroud is one of the few people alive who can genuinely claim to have tested their bodyclocks to the limit.

F The aim is to help us become more efficient.

G An increasing number of people study the state of their bio-rhythms before making their daily plans.

H Man is a prisoner of time.

PART 4

You are going to read about four competitions which offer holidays as prizes. For questions 22–35, choose from the competitions (A–D). Some of the competitions may be chosen more than once. When more than one answer is required, these may be given in any order. There is an example at the beginning (0).
Mark your answers on the separate answer sheet.

Which holiday prize offers you the chance to:

visit a desert?

| 0 | *B* |

go to the seaside?

| 22 | | 23 | |

stay in a new hotel?

| 24 | |

have a chance to exercise?

| 25 | | 26 | |

be sure of seeing some animals?

| 27 | |

look around the city and see something of the countryside?

| 28 | |

stay longer than a week?

| 29 | | 30 | |

Which competition extract:

describes what will happen on the flight?

| 31 | |

says there is more than one prize?

| 32 | |

offers to take the winner on a historical tour as part of the prize

| 33 | |

offers a holiday which includes all food?

| 34 | |

is advertising a particular product?

| 35 | |

A

clearly CANADA

Vancouver is a stylish, metropolitan centre with the scenic Pacific Ocean at its feet and impressive coastal mountains behind. To give you the chance to experience its delights for yourself, *Options* magazine has teamed up with 'Clearly Canadian' – a blend of native Canadian fruit flavours and sparkling water – to bring you this great competition.

The lucky prizewinner and guest will enjoy a fabulous ten-day getaway, flying direct to Vancouver with Canadian Airlines. On board, they will enjoy an in-flight movie while sampling a delicious meal served on real china.

Accommodation for the winner and guest will be at Shangri-La's Pacific Palisades Hotel, one of Vancouver's first-class hotels. They will enjoy a luxury executive suite, with stunning views over the harbour, and use of the hotel's health club and pool. Ten runners-up will receive a bottle of 'Clearly Canadian' and an exclusively designed T-shirt.

While in Vancouver, you will have many opportunities to sample Canadian city life. Browse in fashionable shops, linger in sidewalk cafés or relax on the beach.

Buy this magazine next week and we'll give you the competition details.

B

GO WILD!

NAMIBIA is a country of desert dunes, wide horizons and clear skies. Enter this competition and you and a friend could be on your way.

Your one-week prize holiday begins at Heathrow airport where you will board an Air Namibia plane bound for the capital. Air Namibia Holidays' magnificent Namibia tour will take you straight to the very heart of the country. All travel arrangements will be taken care of – all you have to do is sit back and enjoy the scenery. You'll start with a drive to the Namib Desert Park, then go on to see the pelicans, flamingos and terns at Walvis Bay lagoon, before heading for the coastal resort of Swakopmund.

The highlight of the tour is a safari through Etosha National Park, home to thousands of elephants, zebras, giraffes and antelopes as well as lions, leopards, cheetahs and rhinos.

All meals are included throughout the holiday and you'll stay in some of Namibia's best lodges and camps.

We just ask you to think of

C

WIN A FABULOUS HOLIDAY FOR TWO!

Visit the deserted city of Fatehpur Sikri. Stand back in amazement as you marvel at the wildlife reserves where you'll see exotic birds and possibly even a tiger! These are just some of the sights you'll experience on the thrilling ten-day 'Moghul Highlights' holiday.

The holiday begins with a tour of Old Delhi. Proceeding by road to Agra, you'll stop on the way to see the Tomb of Akbar. Moving on to see Agra Fort and the beautiful Taj Mahal on the banks of the Yamuna River, your group will then explore Akbar's red sandstone city, Fatehpur Sikri, built in 1574. Lunch will be taken in the Keoladeo National Park at Bharatpur, a birdwatcher's paradise.

This fantastic holiday package includes the return flight from Heathrow to Delhi, the holiday tour and insurance. All breakfasts while in India are included but holiday participants will need to buy meals at local restaurants in India.

To find out what you have to do

D

win *a week of luxury in* BUDAPEST

The lucky winner and a friend will fly direct to Budapest International Airport and will then be taken to The Palace Hotel, a luxurious hotel set in its own large park on the banks of the river Danube. The Palace Hotel is just two years old – a modern addition to the ancient skyline.

You'll enjoy five nights' bed and breakfast accommodation in a room that overlooks the river Danube, and will be treated to dinner in the Café Suisse. We have not ordered lunch for you but it is also available in the restaurant.

The week in Budapest can be spent at leisure either relaxing in the hotel and its grounds, or wandering around the superb shopping arcade. Alternatively, The Palace Hotel has extensive health club facilities – including an indoor pool and a free steam bath. If you're feeling really energetic, you could play a game of tennis or jog around the grounds on the two-mile landscaped track.

To make sure you take in some of the sights of Budapest, you may wish to book at very reasonable cost a day's sightseeing with President Holidays.

Look at the next page to see what you have to do.

PAPER 2   WRITING (1 hour 30 minutes)

PART 1

*You **must** answer this question.*

1   You are on holiday at the Bayview Hotel and have decided to come back to
the same place next year. You have kept a diary during your stay. Part of this
is shown below with the holiday advertisement which you cut out. You have
made some notes on the advertisement.

Read the diary and the advertisement. Then write a letter to your friend,
persuading him or her to come with you next year. Use the information given
to say what you could do together.

MONDAY

Sailing – first time for me!

Evening – new Spielberg film

TUESDAY

Coach trip to old town

Evening – disco

Bayview Hotel
Family-run hotel on sea front. Restaurant, bars.

friendly people   *good food*

Write a letter of between **120–180** words in an appropriate style on the next
page. Do not write any addresses.

PART 1

PART 2

*Write an answer to **one** of the questions **2–5** in this part. Write your answer in
120–180 words in an appropriate style on the next page, putting the question
number in the box.*

2   As part of a new series, an educational magazine has invited readers to write
articles called **How and why I started learning English**. Write an **article**
based on your own experience.

3   Your teacher has asked you to write a story which includes the sentence **That
was the moment when I realised I was in the wrong place**. Write your
story.

4   A local newspaper has invited reviews of restaurants from its readers. Write a
report on a visit to **one** local restaurant. Your report should cover the food,
service, decoration and atmosphere of the restaurant, and should also
comment on any problems you experienced.

5   **Background reading texts**

Answer **one** of the following two questions based on your reading of **one** of
the set books (see p.2). Write the title of the book next to the question number
box.

Either **(a)**   Describe some of the most important actions in the book and
explain how they help to develop the story.

or   **(b)**   Would the book make a good film? Say why or why not.

PART 2

Question	

....
....
....
....
....
....
....
....
....
....
....
....
....
....
....
....
....
....
....
....
....
....
....
....
....
....
....
....
....
....

PAPER 3 USE OF ENGLISH (1 hour 15 minutes)

PART 1

For questions **1–15**, *read the text below and decide which answer* **A, B, C** *or* **D** *best fits each space. There is an example at the beginning* **(0)**.
Mark your answers **on the separate answer sheet.**

Example:

0 **A** sigh **B** yawn **C** cough **D** sneeze

0	A	B	C	D
	▬	▭	▭	▭

HELEN AND MARTIN

With a thoughtful **(0)** .... , Helen turned away from the window and walked back to her favourite armchair. **(1)** .... her brother never arrive? For a brief moment, she wondered if she really cared that much.

Over the years Helen had given **(2)** .... waiting for Martin to take an interest in her. Her feelings for him had gradually **(3)** .... until now, as she sat waiting for him, she experienced no more than a sister's **(4)** .... to see what had **(5)** .... of her brother.

Almost without **(6)** .... , Martin had lost his job with a busy publishing company after spending the last eight years in New York as a key figure in the US office. Somehow the two of them hadn't **(7)** .... to keep in touch and, left alone, Helen had slowly found her **(8)** .... in her own judgement growing. **(9)** .... the wishes of her parents, she had left university halfway **(10)** .... her course and now, to the astonishment of the whole family, she was **(11)** .... a fast-growing reputation in the pages of respected art magazines and was actually earning enough to live **(12)** .... from her paintings.

Of course, she **(13)** .... no pleasure in Martin's sudden misfortune, but she couldn't **(14)** .... looking forward to her brother's arrival with **(15)** .... satisfaction at what she had achieved.

1 **A** Could   **B** Should   **C** Would   **D** Ought

2 **A** in   **B** up   **C** out   **D** away

3 **A** depressed   **B** weakened   **C** lowered   **D** fainted

4 **A** wonder   **B** idea   **C** curiosity   **D** regard

5 **A** become   **B** developed   **C** arisen   **D** changed

6 **A** caution   **B** warning   **C** advice   **D** signal

7 **A** minded   **B** concerned   **C** worried   **D** bothered

8 **A** dependence   **B** confidence   **C** certainty   **D** courage

9 **A** Ignoring   **B** Omitting   **C** Avoiding   **D** Preventing

10 **A** along   **B** down   **C** through   **D** across

11 **A** gaining   **B** reaching   **C** starting   **D** opening

12 **A** for   **B** by   **C** with   **D** on

13 **A** made   **B** took   **C** drew   **D** formed

14 **A** help   **B** miss   **C** fail   **D** drop

15 **A** soft   **B** fine   **C** quiet   **D** still

PART 2

*For questions **16–30**, read the text below and think of the word which best fits each space. Use only **one** word in each space. There is an example at the beginning (**0**).*
*Write your word **on the separate answer sheet**.*

Example: | 0 | *most* | 0 |

CYCLING ROUND CORNERS

Taking a corner is one of the **(0)** .... satisfying moves you can make on a bike. It's fun, it's exciting, and it also happens **(16)** .... be one of the hardest things to learn. Even **(17)** .... experienced rider can always **(18)** .... improvements in this area. Good cornering is the ability to cycle through a turn **(19)** .... full control, no matter **(20)** .... the conditions. This might mean racing **(21)** .... high speed down a winding descent, but just **(22)** .... important is the ability to deal with a slow, sharp turn **(23)** .... you are touring with lots of luggage. In **(24)** .... these cases there are some general points to remember.

When going very slowly you can steer through a corner using your hands on the handlebars **(25)** .... , as speed increases, any sudden turning of the front wheel **(26)** .... likely to result in loss of control. To avoid **(27)** .... effect, a bike must be turned by leaning it, by steering with the body instead of the hands. On sharp turns of more **(28)** .... about 70 degrees, even this is **(29)** .... enough: you must also lower your body towards the bike as much as you **(30)** .... to help keep it from slipping out from under you. When you are cornering correctly you will feel very solid. It's a good feeling – exciting but not really dangerous.

PART 3

*For questions **31–40**, complete the second sentence so that it has a similar meaning to the first sentence, using the word given. **Do not change the word given**. You must use between two and five words, including the word given. There is an example at the beginning (**0**).*
*Write **only** the missing words **on the separate answer sheet**.*

Example:

0 I last saw him at my 21st birthday party.
    since

    I .... my 21st birthday party.

The gap can be filled by the words 'haven't seen him since' so you write:

0	*haven't seen him since*	0	0 1 2

31 There's no point in asking George to help.
    worth

    It .... George to help.

32 Harry couldn't get his parents' permission to buy a motorbike.
    let

    Harry's parents .... a motorbike.

33 'Where have I left my sunglasses, David?' asked Susan.
    where

    Susan asked David .... sunglasses.

34 John's behaviour at the party annoyed me.
    John

    I was annoyed by the .... at the party.

35 It's a good thing you lent me the money or I would have had to go to the bank.
    you

    I would have had to go to the bank .... me the money.

36 Matthew didn't listen to what his doctor told him.
notice

Matthew took .... advice.

37 Sheila had to finish the accounts and write several letters as well.
addition

Sheila had to finish the accounts .... several letters.

38 When he was a child in Australia, Mark went swimming almost every day.
his

Mark went swimming almost every day .... in Australia.

39 Let's visit the museum this afternoon.
go

Why .... the museum this afternoon?

40 Valerie found it hard to concentrate on her book because of the noise.
difficulty

Valerie .... her book because of the noise.

*For questions **41–55**, read the text below and look carefully at each line. Some of the lines are correct, and some have a word which should not be there. If a line is correct, put a tick (✓) by the number **on the separate answer sheet**. If a line has a word which should **not** be there, write the word **on the separate answer sheet**. There are two examples at the beginning (**0** and **00**).*

Examples:

0	✓	0
00	*of*	0

A PLACE WORTH VISITING

0	The Welsh National Folk Museum in Cardiff is one of the
00	most interesting of places I've ever visited and it's situated in
41	a very pretty countryside. The museum has collected various
42	buildings from all over the country and brought them together
43	in the grounds of a historic manor house, near where they have
44	been carefully rebuilt one brick by brick to look just like they
45	did in their original position. Then the interiors they have
46	been furnished in period style, and many interesting old tools
47	and other everyday household objects are on the display
48	in this realistic setting. It's fascinating to walk away from
49	building to building, imagining about the way people used to
50	live since years ago. Large families often lived in the tiniest
51	of cottages, sometimes even sharing in the space with the
52	domestic animals which were of such an importance to them.
53	You can go around the manor house as well, but in my opinion
54	there is no little to distinguish this from many other historic
55	houses elsewhere. It does have a much comfortable tea-room,
	however, which is very welcome after all that walking.

PART 5

*For questions **56–65**, read the text below. Use the word given in capitals at the end of each line to form a word that fits in the space in the same line. There is an example at the beginning (**0**). Write your word **on the separate answer sheet**.*

Example:

0	*construction*	0 __ __

THE FUTURE OF TALL BUILDINGS

Architects responsible for the **(0)** .... of many skyscrapers believe **CONSTRUCT**
that a tall building must always have a certain minimum **(56)** .... but **WIDE**
that there is no limit to its absolute **(57)** .... . This means that the **HIGH**
skyscrapers of the future are likely to be even taller.

Engineers agree with this, but there is **(58)** .... over the best shape for **AGREE**
very tall, slim buildings. The effects of wind **(59)** .... mean that **PRESS**
cylindrical designs have enjoyed some **(60)** .... in recent years, and **POPULAR**
these are quite pleasing to the eye. **(61)** .... , however, the ideal **FORTUNATE**
shape is an ugly square with heavily rounded corners.

Would these tall buildings of the future offer more than a **(62)** .... **WONDER**
view? Some believe tall towers could contain all the **(63)** .... for **REQUIRE**
modern living. The **(64)** .... of these vertical villages would travel up **INHABIT**
and down between their home and work zones and would **(65)** .... **RARE**
need to journey to ground level.

PAPER 4   LISTENING (approximately 40 minutes)

PART 1

You will hear people talking in eight different situations.
*For questions **1–8**, choose the best answer **A, B** or **C**.*

1   You are visiting a trade exhibition when you hear a speaker at one of the
stands.
What is he demonstrating?

   A   a watch

   B   a lock

   C   a burglar alarm

      1

2   This girl is talking about a party.
What was it like?

   A   boring

   B   too crowded

   C   noisy

      2

3   Listen to this hotel receptionist talking on the phone.
Who is she talking to?

   A   a friend

   B   a guest

   C   her employer

      3

4   You hear this advertisement on the radio.
Who is it aimed at?

   A   people who have plenty of money

   B   people who might borrow money

   C   people who need to save money

      4

5 Listen to these students talking about their holiday work.
Where are they working?

    A a library

    B an office

    C a shop

	5

6 Listen to this man.
Where has he been?

    A to the gym

    B to the dentist

    C to the barber

	6

7 You hear this woman talking on the radio.
What is she discussing?

    A music

    B a picture

    C architecture

	7

8 You hear this man talking to a shop assistant.
Why is he annoyed?

    A His pen has leaked in his pocket.

    B HIs pen has been repaired recently.

    C His pen was very expensive.

	8

PART 2

You will hear a teacher telling new students about their course.
*For questions **9–18**, listen to what she says and complete the notes.*

Classes in Studio every afternoon

Room 51 on **9** [_____]

On Fridays can use **10** [_____] for private study

Extra courses: Monday **11** [_____]

Tuesday **12** [_____]

Wednesday **13** [_____]

Application forms from **14** [_____]

Saturday course on computer-aided design

Open to **15** [_____] students only

Must provide own **16** [_____]

Short absences, phone **17** [_____]

More than two days, write to **18** [_____]

PART 3

You will hear five people saying thank you.
For questions 19–23, choose which of A–F each speaker is talking about. Use the letters only once. There is one extra letter which you do not need to use.

A   good teaching

B   support in a difficult task

C   a warning

D   a present

E   a piece of information

F   a loan

Speaker 1		**19**
Speaker 2		**20**
Speaker 3		**21**
Speaker 4		**22**
Speaker 5		**23**

PART 4

You will hear a radio discussion about a wildlife park.
For questions 24–30, decide which of the choices A, B or C is the correct answer.

24 Where is South Glen?

   A inside Glenside Park
   B between the park and the main road
   C near the park

	24

25 What does Ian say about Helen's plans?

   A He doesn't like them.
   B He doesn't understand them.
   C He doesn't know what they are.

	25

26 Helen claims that, at present, visitors

   A walk about in large groups.
   B go all over the park.
   C damage the plants.

	26

27 Why is it a problem for the staff to raise young birds?

   A They lack the necessary skills.
   B It costs a lot of money.
   C There isn't the right equipment.

	27

28 Ian thinks it is ridiculous to

   A encourage more visitors.
   B make visitors pay an entrance fee.
   C build fences round the animals.

	28

29 Helen says that fires

   A have been started by accident.
   B are impossible to control.
   C are a possible danger.

	29

30 Ian believes that the villagers nowadays

   A are more aware of the environment than
      their grandparents.
   B show enough respect for the environment.
   C have become careless about the environment.

	30

PAPER 5   SPEAKING (approximately 15 minutes)

Part 1

You tell the examiner about yourself. The examiner may ask you questions such as: Where are you from? How do you usually spend your free time? What are your plans for the future? Your partner does the same.

Part 2

The examiner gives you two pictures to look at and asks you to talk about them for about a minute. Your partner does the same with two different pictures.

Part 3

The examiner gives you a photograph or drawing to look at with your partner. You are asked to solve a problem or come to a decision about something in the picture. For example, you might be asked to decide the best way to use some rooms in a language school. You discuss the problem together.

Part 4

You are asked more questions connected with your discussion in Part 3. For example, you might be asked to talk about the best ways of studying.

Practice Test 4

PAPER 1 READING (1 hour 15 minutes)

PART 1

You are going to read a magazine article about pollution of the atmosphere.
*Choose the most suitable heading from the list (**A–I**) for each part (**1–7**) of the*
article. There is one extra heading which you do not need to use. There is an
*example at the beginning (**0**).*
*Mark your answers **on the separate answer sheet**.*

A	Before ozone existed
B	Repair gets slower
C	People ignore warnings
D	Ozone hole a certainty
E	The future is our responsibility
F	The function of the ozone layer
G	Delayed reactions
H	Humans to blame
I	Strange results

82

The ozone layer
What is it? What is happening to it?

0   ***I***

In September 1982, Dr Joe Farman, a British scientist working in the Antarctic, found that a dramatic change had taken place in the atmosphere above his research station on the ice continent. His instruments, set up to measure the amounts of a chemical called ozone in the atmosphere, seemed to go wild. Over just a few days they recorded that half the ozone had disappeared.

1

He couldn't believe his eyes, so he came back to Britain to get a new instrument to check his findings. But when he returned the following year at the same time, the same thing happened. He had discovered a hole in the ozone layer – an invisible shield in the upper atmosphere – that turned out to extend over an area of the sky as wide as the United States and as deep as Mount Everest is high. When he published his findings in scientific journals, they caused a sensation. Scientists blamed pollution for causing the ozone hole.

2

The ozone layer is between 15 and 40 kilometres up in the atmosphere, higher than most aeroplanes fly. This region contains most of the atmosphere's ozone, which is a special form of the gas oxygen. Ozone has the unique ability to stop certain dangerous invisible rays from the sun from reaching the Earth's surface – rather like a pair of sunglasses filters out bright sunlight. These rays are known as ultra-violet radiation. This damages living cells, causing sunburn and more serious diseases. The ozone layer is vital to life on the surface of the Earth.

3

Until the ozone layer formed, about two thousand million years ago, it was impossible for any living thing to survive on the surface of the planet. All life was deep in the oceans. But once oxygen was formed in the air, and some of that oxygen turned to ozone, plants and animals could begin to move on to land.

4

But now humans are damaging the ozone layer for the first time. In the past ten years, scientists have discovered that some man-made gases, used in everything from refrigerators and aerosols to fire extinguishers, are floating up into the ozone layer and destroying the ozone. The most common of these gases are called chlorofluorocarbons (CFCs).

5

The damage is worst over Antarctica, and near the North Pole, where scientists have seen small holes appear for a short time each spring since 1989. So far, these holes have healed up again within a few weeks by natural processes in the atmosphere that create more ozone. But each year, it seems to take longer for the healing to be completed. Also, all round the planet, there now seems to be less ozone in the ozone layer than even a few years ago.

6

The first new international law to stop people making or using CFCs was the Montreal Protocol, agreed by most of the world's governments in 1987. Since then, there have been new controls on other chemicals that destroy ozone. The problem is that it takes roughly eight years for CFCs, which are released when an old fridge is broken up, to reach the ozone layer. That is why, despite all the cuts, ozone holes were deeper than ever around both the North and South Poles in 1993. Amounts of CFCs in the atmosphere will continue to rise for another five years, say scientists.

7

Every year, the atmosphere will attempt to repair damage to the ozone layer caused by our pollution. But we are stretching its capacity to recover to the limit. If we stop using all ozone-destroying chemicals within the next five years, it is likely to be at least the middle of the 21st century before the ozone hole stops forming over Antarctica each year. And, if we are to survive, we all have to face the problem now.

PART 2

*You are going to read an article about a woman called Rebecca Ridgway. For questions **8–14**, choose the answer (**A, B, C** or **D**) which you think fits best according to the text.*

*Mark your answers **on the separate answer sheet**.*

Tea at Ardmore

To reach Ardmore and take tea with Rebecca Ridgway you must make an expedition; not, perhaps an expedition in the Ridgway class, involving months of painstaking planning, physical training, mental preparation; not, when it's underway, the same degree of discomfort or edge of danger, but a prolonged exercise in transport arrangements in order to reach her crofthouse on a roadless peninsula near Cape Wrath, in the north-west corner of Scotland.

Rebecca does have neighbours; most importantly her parents, John and Marie-Christine Ridgway and one or two other self-sufficient solitaries who have settled in the remains of the crofting community of Ardmore. The Ridgways' extended crofthouse is not only the nerve-centre of the John Ridgway Adventure School, but the living heart of a community whose isolation is intensified by every storm from the Atlantic.

I walk along the peninsula towards the white house above the lake. Although Rebecca now lives in the cottage next door, she is waiting with Marie-Christine in the family kitchen, mugs on the table and kettle on the boil. Mother and daughter share the same slight figures and delicate good looks, but their grace disguises a toughness built up on daily five-mile runs and early morning swims in the freezing waters of the lake.

'Dad's out there somewhere,' says Rebecca, waving a hand at the mountain view, 'with some of his students.' Each year, many of the same people turn up for the Adventure School's women's course of hillwalking and sailing. Ardmore welcomes are always warm, and there is news to exchange; much has happened to the Ridgways since we last met – not least Rebecca's voyage in a canoe round tempestuous Cape Horn. And now, after twenty-five seasons, the family are to close the school for a time and sail away (not exactly round the world, which John and Marie-Christine have already done when they raced their boat *English Rose VII*, or merely across the Atlantic, which John rowed with Chay Blyth in 1966), but round the land mass of South America. All three will make the eighteen-month voyage.

'Dad's been trying to persuade us to do this trip for years, although Mum always swore she'd never sail with him again. He makes everything so stressful and we all get dreadfully seasick. But we need a break from the school.'

The timing, from Rebecca's point of view, couldn't be more perfect. Since she canoed round the Horn and wrote the book which describes that singular adventure she feels 'the pressure is off'. For years she has been set the example of high-achieving parents – the driven, demanding ex-soldier and his deceptively fragile-looking wife, 'who is tougher than any of us, who works harder than any of us, who is my main inspiration' – and now feels she has done the 'something amazing' that was expected of her. 'Cape Horn was Mum's suggestion, although it's Dad who usually sets the toughest challenges.' Marie-Christine says her bright idea subsequently gave her more than a few sleepless nights.

'I suppose I've always been trying to prove something to Dad,' continues Rebecca, 'Not so much seek his approval as get some recognition. When I was younger I was a bit scared of this figure who marched about barking orders. But since we've travelled together – even sharing tents, for heaven's sake – I feel I've

got to know him better.'
   She is more relaxed about the future than she's ever been, less anxious about 'finding some kind of sensible qualification, like physiotherapy' to back up all the skills

90

acquired on land and water, as shepherd, sailor, outdoor pursuits instructor and now writer fighting with a lap-top computer in the South Atlantic to send articles to the *Daily Telegraph.*

95

8 It is a challenge to take tea with Rebecca Ridgway because
   A she lives in a dangerous spot.
   B it is difficult to persuade her to meet people.
   C she expects her guests to be very fit.
   D it is difficult to get to her home.

9 What does 'it' in line 6 refer to?
   A planning
   B tea
   C an exercise
   D an expedition

10 What are we told about Rebecca's home?
   A It is part of a settlement which used to be bigger.
   B It is the only house in the area.
   C It is shared with her parents.
   D It has been damaged in a storm.

11 What has Rebecca gained from the expedition round Cape Horn?
   A She has satisfied her parents' ambitions for her.
   B She has done something which her father was unable to achieve.
   C She has shown that she is stronger than her parents.
   D She has found out that she is a good writer.

12 What is her relationship with her father like?
   A She wishes he were less strict.
   B She wants him to notice her.
   C She is still frightened of him.
   D She wishes he were more like her mother.

13 What do we learn about Marie-Christine?
   A She is not as fit as she used to be.
   B She has never been very keen on sailing.
   C She is stronger than she looks.
   D She has always expected too much of her daughter.

14 How does Rebecca feel about the future?
   A She would like to have a change.
   B She is happy with the way things are going.
   C She wants to qualify as a physiotherapist.
   D She would like to have more time to write.

PART 3

*You are going to read a report of an interview with a film star. Eight sentences have been removed from the interview. Choose from the sentences (**A–I**) the one which fits each gap (**15–21**). There is one extra sentence which you do not need to use. There is an example at the beginning (**0**).*
*Mark your answers **on the separate answer sheet**.*

Having a wonderful time

Judy Sloane meets Hollywood star **Douglas Fairbanks Junior**, son of the famous actor in silent movies. Fairbanks Junior has made an extremely successful career of his own.

Being brought up in a show business family, did you want to be an actor?

Well, it wasn't a show business family. [**0** — *I*] I couldn't help but be aware of it to a certain extent, because people would come around but the talk was very seldom shop-talk.

During your long and successful career you've certainly made the name Fairbanks your own, but when you were starting out was it a nuisance to you to be named after your father?

I think it probably was. It was a mixture in a way. It was useful in having the door open to get interviews, and to be allowed in to talk to the boss. [**15**]

Were you and your father close?

Not at first. We were just shy of each other. I think we were always fond of each other. [**16**] It wasn't until I was in my late twenties that we got to know each other very well.

Was your father a big influence in your life?

Not really, except I certainly took notice of his wonderful good nature with people. [**17**] It was a natural friendliness, and I admired that and I probably wanted to give that same impression when I was young.

Out of all your father's films, do you have a favourite one?

I think my very favourite one is 'Thief Of Baghdad'. It was one of the finest films ever made by anybody. [**18**] He was the guide and more or less the creator.

When did you know that you wanted to become an actor yourself?

When my mother and I were living abroad because it was cheaper, and mother's family had run out of money and we didn't know quite what to do, and somebody offered me a job! **19 [   ]** It was a job at Paramount Pictures to play in a film called 'Stephen Steps Out' for which I got $1,000 a week for two weeks.

Your role as Rupert of Hentzau in 'The Prisoner Of Zenda' was one of your greatest.

It was a wonderful, wonderful part. **20 [   ]** Then I had this offer to come back and do 'Prisoner Of Zenda'. I thought I'd better stick with this new company I'd started. My father was around and he said, 'Don't be a fool, you've got to go back, give up everything and play in "The Prisoner Of Zenda". It's the best part ever written'. And that decided me so I said, 'Yes, I will!'

Do you like the films they're making today?

The films themselves are all right. **21 [   ]** There are still some very fine films that are being made, but some of them are of questionable taste and I blame the public. Being a business and an industry, producers produce what people buy. If the public don't like it, they won't go, and the films will stop being produced.

A The same talents are there, it's the public that has changed.

B He was always very nice to everybody he talked to, and he didn't have to pretend.

C That's when I decided!

D It should have been better.

E But it didn't make the jobs any easier, in fact it probably made them harder, because they expected more than I was able to deliver at a young age.

F We didn't quite know how to show it.

G I think it's a great work of art, and although a lot of people are credited with having a hand in it, everybody did more or less as my father wanted.

H In fact I didn't know whether to accept it or not, because I'd been struggling for years to have my own company in Europe and I was just getting started on that.

I Only my father was in the business, and it wasn't brought home.

PART 4

You are going to read an article about a family trying a vegetarian diet. For questions **22–35**, *choose from the people in the box (***A–E***). Some of the people may be chosen more than once. When more than one answer is required, these may be given in any order.*
*There is an example at the beginning (***0***).*
Mark your answers **on the separate answer sheet**.

A Sue	**B** Michael	**C** Jo	**D** Mary	**E** Robin

Which person:

changed one of the recipes?

0	*A*

doesn't miss meat at all?

22		23	

prefers dishes which are not too spicy?

24	

was keenest to try the diet?

25	

likes dishes to have plenty of taste?

26	

finds the new diet allows less time for doing other things?

27	

misses some of the foods the family no longer eats?

28		29	

has found the experience very rewarding in terms of ideas?

30	

can't eat too much vegetarian food?

31	

already knew quite a lot about healthy eating?   **32**

likes to eat meat sometimes?   **33**   **34**

will probably give up eating fish soon?   **35**

TAKING THE
plunge

If you're thinking about the idea of turning vegetarian but are afraid it may be boring or too expensive, think again. Last October, we challenged a typical meat-eating family to go on a vegetarian diet for at least seven days.

GET SET *A*
Sue Kent, 42, said 'I'm quite health conscious when it comes to food, so we'd already started to cut out red meat.' To start the week, and put everyone in the right frame of mind, Sue prepared a family favourite, vegetarian chilli. The rest of the week followed like a dream. 'The recipes all went down extremely well,' says Sue. 'The tomato and pasta soup was popular, as was the pasta with tomato and mozzarella sauce, although I've altered it, using a vegetarian blue cheese sauce because that's one of our favourites. I've carried on doing fish which most of us like.'

ALL CHANGE!
The Kents were so impressed by the flavours and variety of their new food regime that when the week ended they decided to continue on a largely vegetarian diet.

But making the change wasn't all plain sailing. 'The big drawback is all the preparation involved,' says Sue. 'It takes much longer than before because of all the chopping.'

So do they feel healthier for their new eating habits? 'It's hard to say, but I think on the whole we do,' says Sue. 'I certainly experiment more with my cooking and use many more herbs and spices than I used to. I'm trying out lots of unusual vegetables that I wouldn't have tried before, such as okra. Vegetarian food is so interesting – it's opened my eyes to a whole new world of cooking!'

What's the overall verdict? Here's what each member of the Kent family had to say.

MICHAEL, 46
'I must say I have been quite impressed by some of the recipes Sue has prepared,' says Michael. 'I love curries and other spicy foods, and we have plenty of those. I reckon vegetable curry is every bit as good as meat curry. The one thing I do miss is the chewing you do with meat, something substantial to get your teeth into. If I was out to dinner I don't think I would refuse a steak. I do miss roast lamb but on the whole I think it has been a great success.'

JO, 16
Jo was the main driving force behind the family trying our plan – and the biggest convert, becoming a strict vegetarian after taking up our challenge.

'Jo used to eat chicken, but she doesn't touch meat or fish at all now,' says Sue. 'She doesn't even miss sausages!'

MARY, 81
Michael's mother was the most hesitant about vegetarianism, but nevertheless she tried everything and liked many of the dishes. However, she did find that too much vegetarian food can affect her digestion.

'It's been quite interesting but I wouldn't like to think I was never going to eat meat again,' she says. 'I prefer simpler, plain foods like egg and cheese or fish to the more exotic foods like okra and peppers. I've never liked herbs and spices either, and I'm not much of a pasta fan.'

SUE, 42
'I'd quite happily never eat meat again, although I'd find it hard to go without fish.'

ROBIN, 2
Robin currently eats fish but he doesn't really care for it so Sue expects he'll be a total vegetarian before long. 'Apart from that, he's not a fussy eater – on a good day he'll eat anything,' says Sue. 'He loves pasta, and vegetable soup goes down well.'

PAPER 2   WRITING (1 hour 30 minutes)

PART 1

*You **must** answer this question.*

1   You are a student at the Swansea College of Higher Education and are the
    secretary of the History Society. You have invited someone called Mr
    Stephens to speak to the Society, but have just realised that you won't be
    able to meet his train which arrives at 4.45. Your diary, a notice about his visit,
    and a map are shown below.

    Look at the diary, the notice and the map. Then write a letter to Mr Stephens
    using all the relevant information. Apologise for not being able to meet the train,
    explain why and suggest how he should get to the college from the station.

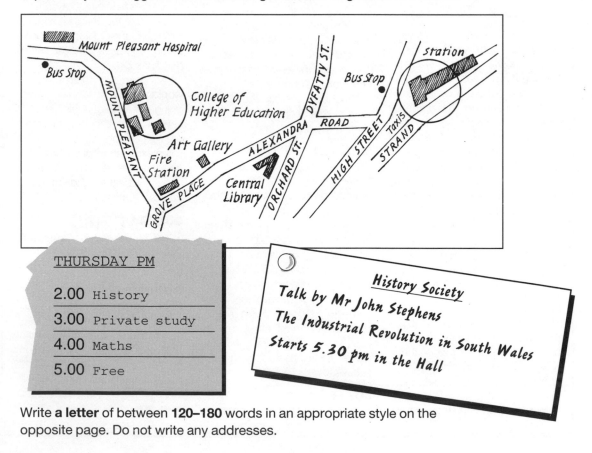

Write **a letter** of between **120–180** words in an appropriate style on the
opposite page. Do not write any addresses.

PART 1

PART 2

*Write an answer to **one** of the questions 2–5 in this part. Write your answer in 120–180 words in an appropriate style on the opposite page, putting the question number in the box.*

2   Your penfriend in Britain asks the following question in his or her latest letter:

I'd like to try preparing a traditional dish from your country. Can you tell me how to do it?

Briefly **describe a typical dish** in your country and give instructions on how to prepare and serve it.

3   A local English-language paper runs a readers' column called **My big mistake**. Write a **story** for the column, describing the circumstances and effects of your mistake, and explaining why it happened.

4   Your teacher has asked you to write about two photographs from your family album which are of particular importance to you. **Describe** what the pictures show and what memories they bring back for you.

5   **Background reading texts**

Answer **one** of the following two questions based on your reading of **one** of the set books (see p.2). Write the title of the book next to the question number box.

Either   **(a)**   Describe a moment which changes the course of the story and say why you think it is particularly important.

or   **(b)**   Choose one of the important relationships in the book and describe how it develops.

PART 2

Question	

....
....
....
....
....
....
....
....
....
....
....
....
....
....
....
....
....
....
....
....
....
....
....
....
....
....
....

PAPER 3   USE OF ENGLISH (1 hour 15 minutes)

*For questions **1–15**, read the text below and decide which answer **A, B, C** or **D**
best fits each space. There is an example at the beginning (**0**).
Mark your answers **on the separate answer sheet**.*

Example:
0   A descends   **B** falls   **C** drops   **D** jumps

0	A	B	C	D
	—			

ANGER ON THE ROADS

The anger that **(0)** .... on people when they get behind the steering wheel of a car
used to be **(1)** .... as a joke. But the laughter is getting noticeably quieter **(2)** .... that
the problem has become increasingly widespread.

(3) .... in a traffic jam, with family cars inching their **(4)** .... past, the driver of a fast
sports car begins to lose his temper. **(5)** .... the capabilities of his car, there is
nothing he can do. The **(6)** .... is anger.

Many people live in **(7)** .... of losing control. This is true of many situations but
driving is a good example. People think that the car might not start, it might break
(8) .... , or someone might run into it. Before anything even happens, people have
worked themselves up into a **(9)** .... of anxiety. And when something does happen,
they're **(10)** .... to explode. In fact, it's their very anxiety about losing control that
(11) .... them lose control.

This isn't to **(12)** .... that all offenders have psychological problems or drive
powerful sports cars. In fact, most of them are **(13)** .... ordinary human beings who
have no history of violence. There is **(14)** .... something deep in our nature that
(15) .... when we start up a car engine.

1   **A** found   **B** thought   **C** treated   **D** intended

2   **A** once   **B** even   **C** since   **D** now

3   **A** Set   **B** Stuck   **C** Held   **D** Fixed

4   **A** path   **B** way   **C** course   **D** route

5   **A** However   **B** Besides   **C** Although   **D** Despite

6   **A** outcome   **B** event   **C** issue   **D** effect

7   **A** worry   **B** fright   **C** fear   **D** concern

8   **A** up   **B** down   **C** out   **D** off

9   **A** state   **B** condition   **C** feeling   **D** case

10 **A** good   **B** prepared   **C** near   **D** ready

11 **A** causes   **B** leads   **C** makes   **D** forces

12 **A** inform   **B** say   **C** tell   **D** announce

13 **A** purely   **B** fully   **C** exactly   **D** perfectly

14 **A** openly   **B** directly   **C** clearly   **D** frankly

15 **A** excites   **B** awakens   **C** disturbs   **D** upsets

*For questions **16–30**, read the text below and think of the word which best fits
each space. Use only **one** word in each space. There is an example at the
beginning (**0**).*
*Write your word **on the separate answer sheet**.*

Example:	0	*to*	0 ▭ ▭

MISSION TO MARS

The Americans are keen to win the race **(0)** .... send human beings to Mars. In 1992,
the new boss of NASA*, Dan Goldin, called on the American people to be the first to
send explorers to **(16)** .... planet in the solar system. He reminded them **(17)** .... the
symbolic gift carried to the moon and back by the Apollo 11 mission. It bears **(18)** ....
message intended for the crew of the first spaceship to visit Mars. Goldin thinks
(19) .... is time to begin the preparations **(20)** .... this historic journey. His speech
echoed the words of the President, **(21)** .... promised that in 2019, 50 years after Neil
Armstrong **(22)** .... the first man to set foot on the Moon, the first astronaut **(23)** ....
stand on Mars.

(24) .... the end of the twentieth century, various unmanned spaceships will **(25)** ....
thoroughly investigated the surface of the planet. But, however clever a robot
(26) .... be, it cannot match the type of information **(27)** .... can be gained from direct
human experience. The first geologist on the moon, Harrison Schmitt, was **(28)** .... of
interpreting the story of the landscape on the spot. **(29)** .... humans walk on the red
deserts of Mars, we will not be able to determine the history of this frozen world
(30) .... any detail.

* The North American Space Agency

PART 3

*For questions **31–40**, complete the second sentence so that it has a similar meaning to the first sentence, using the word given. **Do not change the word given**. You must use between two and five words, including the word given. There is an example at the beginning (**0**).*
*Write **only** the missing words **on the separate answer sheet**.*

Example:

0   I last saw him at my 21st birthday party.
   since

   I .... my 21st birthday party.

The gap can be filled by the words 'haven't seen him since' so you write:

0	*haven't seen him since*	0	0 1 2

---

31 'Why don't you wait by the phone box, Brenda?' said Leslie.
   Brenda

   Leslie suggested .... by the phone box.

32 Although he overslept, Clive wasn't late for work.
   up

   Despite .... on time, Clive wasn't late for work.

33 I haven't eaten food like this before.
   time

   This is the .... this sort of food.

34 After a long chase, the police finally succeeded in arresting the thief.
   to

   After a long chase, the police finally .... the thief.

35 Diane was supposed to write to her parents last week.
   ought

   Diane .... to her parents last week.

36 His handwriting is so small I can hardly read it.
such

He .... I can hardly read it.

37 Somebody has to pick the visitors up from the airport.
up

The visitors .... from the airport.

38 I wish I hadn't told him what we were planning to do this evening.
regret

I .... for this evening.

39 Everyone was surprised to see Geoff leave the party early.
surprise

To .... the party early.

40 All the witnesses said the accident was my fault.
blame

All the witnesses said that .... the accident.

PART 4

*For questions **41–55**, read the text below and look carefully at each line. Some of the lines are correct, and some have a word which should not be there. If a line is correct, put a tick (✓) by the number **on the separate answer sheet**. If a line has a word which should **not** be there, write the word **on the separate answer sheet**. There are two examples at the beginning (**0** and **00**).*

Examples:

0	*to*	0
00	✓	0

A MUCH-IMPROVED JOURNEY

0	Shortly after reaching to Weymouth on the south coast of England
00	on holiday, we caught sight of a small white dot on the horizon,
41	moving at an amazing speed. Surely it couldn't be a ship going so
42	fast? We thought it might still be a trick of the light, but as the shape
43	came closer, it was clear so that we had not been mistaken: it was
44	indeed some sort of a ship and it was travelling very much faster
45	than a normal boat could ever have done in similar conditions.
46	It turned out as to be the new high-speed ferry to the Channel
47	Islands, which could reach Guernsey in just over the two hours. This
48	seemed incredible since the last time when we had visited the island,
49	it had taken us for five hours to get there, but now, with this faster
50	service, a day trip it was clearly a real possibility and we decided to
51	buy tickets for the next day. It also meant getting to the harbour by six
52	o'clock but it was certainly worth making the effort to get up early.
53	The weather was fine and the ferry lived well up to its claims for a
54	comfortable crossing. By half past nine we were relaxing ourselves in
55	a Guernsey café, enjoying a leisurely breakfast and looking out across
	the sea.

*For questions **56–65**, read the text below. Use the word given in capitals at the end of each line to form a word that fits in the space in the same line. There is an example at the beginning (**0**). Write your word **on the separate answer sheet**.*

Example:

0	*marvellous*	0

THE ABC OF COOKING

It's a **(0)** .... idea for children to do some cooking at an early
age. Generally **(56)** .... , most children can't wait to help in the
kitchen and love getting involved in the **(57)** .... of their meals.
They should be **(58)** .... to do so, and care should be taken to
(59) .... they enjoy the experience. It is important to show them
how to do things **(60)** .... but they shouldn't be criticised too much.
Although the finished result may not be quite to your **(61)** .... , the
young cook will undoubtedly find it quite the **(62)** .... food he or
she has ever eaten.

Kitchens can, of course, be **(63)** .... places and so the absolute
(64) .... of keeping an eye on children at all times cannot be
emphasised too **(65)** .... . Sharp knives, for example, should be
avoided until children are old enough to handle them safely.

MARVEL
SPEAK
PREPARE
COURAGE
SURE
CORRECT
LIKE
TASTY

DANGER
IMPORTANT
HEAVY

PAPER 4   LISTENING (approximately 40 minutes)

PART 1

You will hear people talking in eight different situations.
For questions **1–8**, *choose the best answer* **A, B** *or* **C**.

1   These women are talking about a colleague.
    What do they feel about his behaviour?

    A   It was typical of him.

    B   It had improved.

    C   It reminded them of someone else.

    `[1]`

2   This man is talking about a sports event.
    What happened to his team?

    A   They won.

    B   They did better than he'd hoped.

    C   They were very unlucky.

    `[2]`

3   Listen to this man telephoning someone about his washing machine.
    Who is he talking to?

    A   an engineer

    B   a friend

    C   the shop he bought it from

    `[3]`

4   You switch on the radio and hear this report.
    Where is it coming from?

    A   a market

    B   a concert hall

    C   a racetrack

    `[4]`

5 You hear this man talking about his bad back.
How did he injure it?

    A   in a road accident

    B   by lifting something

    C   in a fight

	5

6 You overhear these people talking about a book.
What sort of book is it?

    A   a guidebook

    B   a history book

    C   a novel

	6

7 Listen to this woman who has just arrived at a meeting.
Why is she late?

    A   The weather was bad.

    B   There was a traffic jam.

    C   She crashed her car.

	7

8 At the sports club you hear these people discussing an exercise.
What is its purpose?

    A   to help you lose weight

    B   to make you relax

    C   to strengthen the stomach muscles

	8

PART 2

You will hear part of a radio programme about holidays.
*For questions **9–18**, complete the grid.*

	Eastingham	Brant	Faresey
Main attraction	9	13	16
Size	10	14	
Best transport to get there	11	15	17
Best time of year	12		18

PART 3

You will hear five people talking about clothes.
*For questions **19–23**, choose from the list **A–F** what each speaker is talking about.*
Use the letters only once. There is one extra letter which you do not need to use.

A a hat

B a shirt

Speaker 1	19
Speaker 2	20
Speaker 3	21
Speaker 4	22
Speaker 5	23

C an overcoat

D a suit

E a sock

F a boot

PART 4

You will hear two friends discussing evening study courses.
For questions **24–30**, *decide which course each statement refers to.*
Mark   **A** *for Art*
     or   **C** *for Computers*
     or   **S** *for Spanish*

24   You must book a place on this course.

	24

25   Polly already knows this subject.

	25

26   This course is taught by a qualified teacher.

	26

27   There's an extra charge for this course.

	27

28   This course lasts for two terms.

	28

29   Students work hard on this course.

	29

30   Polly would do this course if she had time.

	30

PAPER 5 SPEAKING (approximately 15 minutes)

Part 1

You tell the examiner about yourself. The examiner may ask you questions such as: Where are you from? How do you usually spend your free time? What are your plans for the future? Your partner does the same.

Part 2

The examiner gives you two pictures to look at and asks you to talk about them for about a minute. Your partner does the same with two different pictures.

Part 3

The examiner gives you a photograph or drawing to look at with your partner. You are asked to solve a problem or come to a decision about something in the picture. For example, you might be asked to decide the best way to use some rooms in a language school. You discuss the problem together.

Part 4

You are asked more questions connected with your discussion in Part 3. For example, you might be asked to talk about the best ways of studying.

CAMBRIDGE
EXAMINATIONS, CERTIFICATES AND DIPLOMAS
ENGLISH AS A FOREIGN LANGUAGE

University of Cambridge
Local Examinations Syndicate
International Examinations

Examination Details	9999/01 99/D99
Examination Title	First Certificate in English
Centre/Candidate No.	AA999/9999
Candidate Name	A.N. EXAMPLE

• Sign here if the details above are correct

X

- -
• Tell the Supervisor now if the details above
  are not correct

Candidate Answer Sheet: FCE Paper 1 Reading

Use a pencil

Mark ONE letter for each
question.

For example, if you think **B** is
the right answer to the
question, mark your answer
sheet like this:

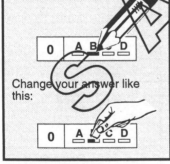

0	A B̶ ̶ D

Change your answer like
this:

0	A ̶ C D

1	A B C D E F G H I
2	A B C D E F G H I
3	A B C D E F G H I
4	A B C D E F G H I
5	A B C D E F G H I

6	A B C D E F G H I
7	A B C D E F G H I
8	A B C D E F G H I
9	A B C D E F G H I
10	A B C D E F G H I
11	A B C D E F G H I
12	A B C D E F G H I
13	A B C D E F G H I
14	A B C D E F G H I
15	A B C D E F G H I
16	A B C D E F G H I
17	A B C D E F G H I
18	A B C D E F G H I
19	A B C D E F G H I
20	A B C D E F G H I

21	A B C D E F G H I
22	A B C D E F G H I
23	A B C D E F G H I
24	A B C D E F G H I
25	A B C D E F G H I
26	A B C D E F G H I
27	A B C D E F G H I
28	A B C D E F G H I
29	A B C D E F G H I
30	A B C D E F G H I
31	A B C D E F G H I
32	A B C D E F G H I
33	A B C D E F G H I
34	A B C D E F G H I
35	A B C D E F G H I

You may photocopy this page.

CAMBRIDGE
EXAMINATIONS, CERTIFICATES AND DIPLOMAS
ENGLISH AS A FOREIGN LANGUAGE

University of Cambridge
Local Examinations Syndicate
International Examinations

Examination Details	9999/03	99/D99
Examination Title	First Certificate in English	
Centre/Candidate No.	AA999/9999	
Candidate Name	A.N. EXAMPLE	

• Sign here if the details above are correct

X

• Tell the Supervisor now if the details above
  are not correct

Candidate Answer Sheet: FCE Paper 3 Use of English

Use a pencil

For **Part 1**: Mark ONE letter for each question.

For example, if you think **C** is the
right answer to the question,
mark your answer sheet like this:

0	A B C D

For **Parts 2, 3, 4** and **5**: Write your
answers in the spaces next to the
numbers like this:

0	example

Part 1				
1	A	B	C	D
2	A	B	C	D
3	A	B	C	D
4	A	B	C	D
5	A	B	C	D
6	A	B	C	D
7	A	B	C	D
8	A	B	C	D
9	A	B	C	D
10	A	B	C	D
11	A	B	C	D
12	A	B	C	D
13	A	B	C	D
14	A	B	C	D
15	A	B	C	D

Part 2	Do not write here
16	16
17	17
18	18
19	19
20	20
21	21
22	22
23	23
24	24
25	25
26	26
27	27
28	28
29	29
30	30

Turn
over
for
Parts
3 - 5
→

You may photocopy this page.

© UCLES/K&J

Part 3		Do not write here		
31		31 0 ⊑	1 ⊑	2 ⊑
32		32 0 ⊑	1 ⊑	2 ⊑
33		33 0 ⊑	1 ⊑	2 ⊑
34		34 0 ⊑	1 ⊑	2 ⊑
35		35 0 ⊑	1 ⊑	2 ⊑
36		36 0 ⊑	1 ⊑	2 ⊑
37		37 0 ⊑	1 ⊑	2 ⊑
38		38 0 ⊑	1 ⊑	2 ⊑
39		39 0 ⊑	1 ⊑	2 ⊑
40		40 0 ⊑	1 ⊑	2 ⊑

Part 4		Do not write here
41		⊑ 41 ⊑
42		⊑ 42 ⊑
43		⊑ 43 ⊑
44		⊑ 44 ⊑
45		⊑ 45 ⊑
46		⊑ 46 ⊑
47		⊑ 47 ⊑
48		⊑ 48 ⊑
49		⊑ 49 ⊑
50		⊑ 50 ⊑
51		⊑ 51 ⊑
52		⊑ 52 ⊑
53		⊑ 53 ⊑
54		⊑ 54 ⊑
55		⊑ 55 ⊑

Part 5		Do not write here
56		⊑ 56 ⊑
57		⊑ 57 ⊑
58		⊑ 58 ⊑
59		⊑ 59 ⊑
60		⊑ 60 ⊑
61		⊑ 61 ⊑
62		⊑ 62 ⊑
63		⊑ 63 ⊑
64		⊑ 64 ⊑
65		⊑ 65 ⊑

CAMBRIDGE
EXAMINATIONS, CERTIFICATES AND DIPLOMAS
ENGLISH AS A FOREIGN LANGUAGE

University of Cambridge
Local Examinations Syndicate
International   Examinations

X

Examination Details	9999/04	99/D99
Examination Title	First Certificate in English	
Centre/Candidate No.	AA999/9999	
Candidate Name	A.N. EXAMPLE	

• Sign here if the details above are correct

• Tell the Supervisor now if the details above
  are not correct

Candidate Answer Sheet: FCE Paper 4 Listening

Mark test version below

A   B   C   D   E

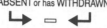

Use a pencil

For **Parts 1** and **3**:
Mark ONE letter for
each question.

For example, if you
think **B** is the right
answer to the
question, mark your
answer sheet like this:

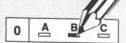

0	A	B	C

For **Parts 2** and **4**:
Write your answers in
the spaces next to the
numbers like this:

0	example

Part 1

1	A	B	C
2	A	B	C
3	A	B	C
4	A	B	C
5	A	B	C
6	A	B	C
7	A	B	C
8	A	B	C

Part 2

	Do not write here
9	▭ 9 ▭
10	▭ 10 ▭
11	▭ 11 ▭
12	▭ 12 ▭
13	▭ 13 ▭
14	▭ 14 ▭
15	▭ 15 ▭
16	▭ 16 ▭
17	▭ 17 ▭
18	▭ 18 ▭

Part 3

19	A	B	C	D	E	F
20	A	B	C	D	E	F
21	A	B	C	D	E	F
22	A	B	C	D	E	F
23	A	B	C	D	E	F

Part 4

	Do not write here
24	▭ 24 ▭
25	▭ 25 ▭
26	▭ 26 ▭
27	▭ 27 ▭
28	▭ 28 ▭
29	▭ 29 ▭
30	▭ 30 ▭

You may photocopy this page.

© UCLES/K&J